Praise for
Intrinsic Work

———————————————

"I love the book. I truly do. The in-depth anecdotal foundation of how you improved your work life and time management was compelling."
—**Melvin**

"The direct style and informative content made it a page-turner. I really can do with a properly structured intrinsic workday. We have countless useless meetings, and most important of all, I also need a proper downtime to recharge. Every solution, every practice felt very doable ... many actionable strategies in the book that can no doubt change a person for the better. Very eye-opening for me personally. Overall, a very informative and enjoyable experience." —**Pragna.J.**

"I was on board right from the beginning. The language was easy to read and understand, the flow was great, and the content was informative. Direct and to the point. Every topic and every section had something important to share ... a lot of information that is not just useful but crucial ... convinced that it will be very helpful in practice in real life. A very eye-opening experience. And most of all, it was a fun experience." —**Sidd. J.**

"The framework was ingestible in an easy way. Seems like a great method and I can totally see how this can make a person a more efficient worker! In addition to all the examples throughout the chapters, the case studies are great! It really helped provide a great example of how we can truly implement the Intrinsic Work System." —**Diana**

"Easy to follow and well laid out. My favorite part which I am going to implement right away is the blocking of my days into more focused chunks." —**Pat**

"Thank you … There are lots of people out there with advice on productivity and success that generally include things like waking up at 5 a.m. in the morning, or starting the day with the meditation, not generally helpful, while this book is!" —**Olga**

INTRINSIC WORK

Also by Andrew Camp

Intrinsic Work the Application
Intrinsic Work the Course

Available at
www.MyIntrinsicWork.com

Achieve More, Work Less,
and Enjoy Life

INTRINSIC
WORK

A Flexible System That Can Help
Most People Up-Level Their Work Life

ANDREW CAMP

INTRINSIC
PUBLISHING

For information about special discounts for bulk purchases or author interviews, appearances, and speaking engagements please contact:

Info@MyIntrinsicLife.com

First Edition

ISBN hardcover	979-8-9925971-2-7
ISBN paperback	979-8-9925971-0-3
ISBN eBook	979-8-9925971-1-0
ISBN audiobook	979-8-9925971-3-4

Library of Congress Control Number 2025902639

Edited by Jennifer Eaton and Robin Noelle.
Interior design and production by Rodney Miles
Cover design by Andrew Camp
Images © Andrew Camp
Avatar images courtesy of www.PixaBay.com

"There is only one success,
to be able to spend your life in your own way."

—Christopher Morley

To my father, the hardest worker I knew.

Contents

Our lives are busier than ever. You will gain control of it all and enjoy a more fulfilling life using our high-performance toolkit! Intrinsic introduces and combines adaptable best practices that will make you wildly productive. Use it like I do, to achieve more, work less, and enjoy life.

Preface

WRITING THIS BOOK has been interesting. It was never in my original goals and I didn't even know I was writing it. My background is in corporate finance, but I have always loved life efficiencies. If I can make something take less time or cost less money while I enjoy the same quality results, that is a win for me!

When I worked at Kaiser Hospital answering phones in college, I automated the preparation of our on-call schedule. It went from an error-prone process that took hours to populate, to a nearly error-free schedule that took 10 minutes to fill in. Easier, faster, higher quality. I loved it.

While I automated a lot of my professional work as well, during the pandemic I picked up a second remote role. The cash was nice, it helped me buy my first house, but the workload was insane.

I started reading books on subjects from efficiency to psychology on a quest to help me juggle it all—the best ones are cited in this book. The result is what I call my *master's degree in productivity* and if it had a thesis, it would be this Intrinsic system.

The system started as a crude Excel file that helped me manage time and tasks. It was ugly, but it definitely helped, which inspired me to grow it, including goals, weekly planning, lists, and other helpful areas.

The results were evident. I squashed two and at times three roles in my 9a-5p workday, while also writing this book and pursuing other passion projects. I figured if QuickBooks can help most people manage their business, then Intrinsic can help most people manage their life. I wanted to share that with others.

The first step I did was documenting how it all worked so I could get it out of the ugly Excel and into a real application. In addition to writing about the mechanical Excel logic, the bare necessity for a coder, I discussed the underlying logic from what I learned, along with tips for success. In the end, it was way too much writing for an application story board, but as I was preparing to chop it down, it looked like I had a framework for a book.

I started researching how to write a book. The most obvious first step was drafting my first version, which I did over several months. The next step suggested by the internet was paying someone for a professional edit. *Oh my, that first draft was ugly.* I ended up doing five edits with three professionals, with each edit adding tremendous value and perspective.

Of course, I was writing this book and making these edits, using the Intrinsic Work approach. Even with several roles, you'll learn that they don't require every moment of your big brain mode.

My hope is that you experience life changing results from the system. Become more productive, and use it to achieve more, work less, and enjoy life.

Andrew

Introduction

[1]

Welcome

ARE YOU LOOKING for upward trajectory, better work-life balance, a career change? Or maybe some combination? With the right systems helping you, they're all achievable.

Are you tired of missing out on birthday parties, weddings, and family picnics? Are you tired of not having energy left over after work to pursue passions, or endlessly working but never reaching the desired results?

I've been there. But notice I wrote that in the past tense... BEEN there. And you will be, too.

This book is for just about anyone who works. Those who have more freedom with their time and what they work on day-to-day, will benefit most. I'm in management and work from home. My day is generally spent on long transactions, such as fundraising or selecting a new business system, a few transactions per year. Conversely, an accounts payable person who works on-site, will have less time flexibility and will be expected to produce many, sometimes hundreds of transactions per day. It's actually "easier" to improve things for higher level roles.

With that said, anyone who works and would like to get more out of it, will find value somewhere in the system. Writing goals to see opportunities, planning tasks and getting well organized, adopting techniques to drive daily momentum, all this will help just about anyone.

Different roles allow you to apply the Intrinsic system better than others, but they all can benefit, especially if you are looking for upward trajectory. Regardless if you're a CFO or an accounts payable clerk, a superintendent or a classroom teacher, a VP of Sales or a customer service rep, the information and exercises in this book will help you feel more in control of work.

My goal is to make you more productive so you can achieve more and/or work less while having more time and energy to spend on your relationships, hobbies, and whatever your passions are outside of work.

An *intrinsic order* is a framework designed to capture everything in its domain. The Periodic Table of the Elements does this for matter. It has a place for every type, and even predicted some that hadn't been found yet. For the sake of this exercise, we'll use a system to capture everything related to your work.

Find enjoyment if you're looking for something new. Achieve results you didn't think were possible. Achieve more. Work less.

Intrinsic Work is nothing new. The magic comes from combining proven methods that inspire, motivate, and most importantly, get it into regular practice where the real results are made.

The Four Parts of the Intrinsic Work System include:

1. **Time Habits**: Time is a powerful but limited resource. Learn to master time and achieve significant gains with less effort.

2. **Big Goals**: Goals inspire action. Identify what truly matters and design a path to accomplish your dreams.

3. **Levered Tasks**: Tasks are the steps to achieve your big goals. You'll achieve milestones faster with research and aligning these levered tasks with their best time habit.

4.   **Drive Momentum**: Momentum helps us stay on track daily and over the long haul. Here we leverage common tools to make big gains easier. Significant results are not measured by personal struggle or seat-hours.

This framework can be adopted at whatever speed feels suitable for you and at whatever scope. My goal is that you have some form of lasting "positive material change," whatever that means to you.

I created this system during the pandemic when life got weird and work got busier. I sought ways to be more effective with my time, and the resulting framework helped me with work and all facets of life. If you only adopt any one part of the book, things will improve for you. Adopting all of it unlocks the magic.

My life is better with this system running, and I believe yours will be too. There will be clear *before Intrinsic* and *after Intrinsic* markers in your life.

I've started with a focus on work because it is often the largest occupier of our waking time and energy. Work satisfaction, performance, and compensation significantly impact our lives. So we solve it first. My companion book, *Intrinsic Life*, applies the framework you'll read about, to your entire life. This includes spirituality, living healthier, rediscovering what brings you joy, and cultivating stronger relationships along with discussing business and personal finance goals. There is an overview at the end of this book.

You can accomplish big things. We may have different-sized hills to climb, but success is within everyone's reach. Having a system that works for you makes a dramatic difference in your performance and day-to-day happiness on your way there.

On a personal note, I love to hear feedback, and it informs the continuous improvement of the system. Please let me know how *Intrinsic Work* has impacted your life.

Thank you,
Andrew Camp

[2]

"Intrinsic Work" Overview

BEING COGNIZANT OF the work system will create options. You can use it to find new trajectories and increase output. You can pursue higher earnings or an outstanding work-life balance or some combination.

This may seem like an impossible dream to some, but combining time, goals, tasks, and drive creates an unstoppable productivity wheel, that will make you capable of producing more than most people.

Let's take a closer look at the four parts of the *Intrinsic Work* system.

The first part, time habits are the most critical component of the system. It's hard to accomplish much without time. This section introduces a few standard blocks of time that fit most jobs. You may have others, but the point is to be cognizant that our days consist of different types of time. Here are the "stock" work-related ***time habits***:

- *Focused time*: Achieve more with less effort during this long-duration, uninterrupted time.

- *Unfocused time*: Never get behind on the small stuff during this short-burst, yet effective time.

- *Meetings*: Maximize their productivity or get rid of them all together! We'll show you how.

- *Downtime:* It's proven to increase performance, so enjoy disconnected lunches and breaks!

These generic descriptions can be molded around most jobs. The point is to be cognizant that there are common recurring chunks of time. Some are better suited for some tasks than others. As a result, some *time habits* are more valuable than others. Their timing and recurrence throughout your days, weeks, and months dramatically impact your productivity.

As mentioned, some roles are more difficult to structure than others. A regional manager at UPS who works in an office can structure their day much easier, than the driver who is out delivering packages. While the driver can't control their time as much, they can definitely set some goals and look for ways to achieve them.

The second part, big goals are proven to help you succeed. Goals guide you to where you're heading and help you identify opportunities when they present themselves. This could be growing your career, achieving a better work-life balance, or changing to a new profession. We set work goals (other than retiring haha) from far to near. *Big goals* are broken into three phases:

- *Long-term goals: Dream big! What situation would make you happy years from now?*

- *Component goals: Dream specific. What possible sub-goals might help get you there?*

- *Annual goals: Dream attainable. What can you do this year to chip away at the sub-goals?*

The **long-term goal** is big and audacious. It serves as your North Star and will evolve. **Component goals** break the North Star into more specific pieces. **Annual goals** break the pieces into short-term, attainable goals. This helps your brain connect your day-to-day efforts with your bigger purpose. Simply writing your goals will improve your productivity by guiding your intention and helping you find opportunities and it only takes a few minutes.

The third part, levered tasks are the actions we take each day to achieve our goals. This is what you do in the moment to make progress. The better your tasks are designed, and aligned with your time habits, the faster your goals will be achieved and probably exceeded. Task planning has two oscillating steps:

- *Uplevel tasks with research. Others have likely attempted something similar, see what they did before diving in.*

- *Align the tasks with your Time Habits to help with prioritization.*

Research involves looking for the best approach to achieve your **annual goals** and learning from others who have come before you. This leads to identifying the best tasks you can do, within the various **time habits**. Some tasks require big brain focus, while others just need a few moments, but everything must get done.

The fourth part, driving momentum helps you push along day-to-day and over the long haul. Learning about **time habits**, writing **big goals**, and even identifying **levered tasks** is the easy part! Doing it consistently is the hard part. **Driving momentum** consists of the following pieces:

- *Daily planning: Real-world time management for busy people, here we introduce the Super Day template.*

- *Accountability*: Proven methods to stay on track, measure what matters.

- *Helpful tools*: Digital and analog helpers to make all this easier and increase your success!

Daily planning uses the **Super Day** format to plan your day by **time habits** and **levered tasks**, in consideration of your real life responsibilities.

Accountability is about finding a cheerleader who will encourage you. In the beginning, that cheerleader will be *you.* Along the way you can expand this to include other people.

Helpful tools are strategies to make organization easier and to put your mind at ease after hours.

Each piece of **Intrinsic Work** is valuable on its own. Implement any of them, and your work life will improve. Implementing all of them will deliver exponential productivity. Use it to achieve more, work less, and enjoy life.

Take a deep breath. I know this sounds like a lot, and it is. But it's not as overwhelming a change as it first appears. We break it down to manageable steps that can be adopted and whatever pace and scale feels right to you.

Ready to take control of your work life? Great! Let's go!

Part 1:
Time Habits

[3]

"When"

Nothing is more important than time; learn to harness it!

TIME IS OUR most valuable resource. Without it, nothing else matters. When was the last time you missed a school play, a friend's special event, or missed your team making the winning goal?

Yesterday? You're not alone.

Working parents often miss their children's events, busy friends promise to make it next time, and our hobbies fall to the wayside. We're not happy about it, but the work must get done. The better we control work time, the more time we have for the people and activities we love.

Everyone has a finite twenty-four hours in a day. These twenty-four hours are augmented by challenges, responsibilities, and everyday life. It's a proven fact that structuring your work time will make you more productive.

Take two identical people with the same jobs, capabilities, and challenges. They spend equal time on tasks, on Facebook, in meetings, talking to co-workers, taking breaks, checking emails, etc. Yet, their workdays can have entirely different outcomes based solely on how they structure their time. As mentioned, I'm writing this from the perspective of a management office who has a lot of control over their time. However, even my personal trainer found value in the concepts and applied them in a health club setting. Regardless of what you do, be cognizant of time, it is your most valuable resource. Especially if you are looking for work to improve.

The Intrinsic Workday promotes concentrating how we spend our time. The result is increasing our output with the same hours spent. The key is to reduce the number of times we switch between dissimilar time habits and their tasks. Every time you switch, you reduce your productivity. A quick phone call or question from a co-worker might only take a few minutes of clock time, but it burns immense amounts of productive time as you engage, disengage, and re-engage.

According to the American Psychological Society's article, "Multitasking: Switching Costs," task switching can cost you up to 40% of your productivity.

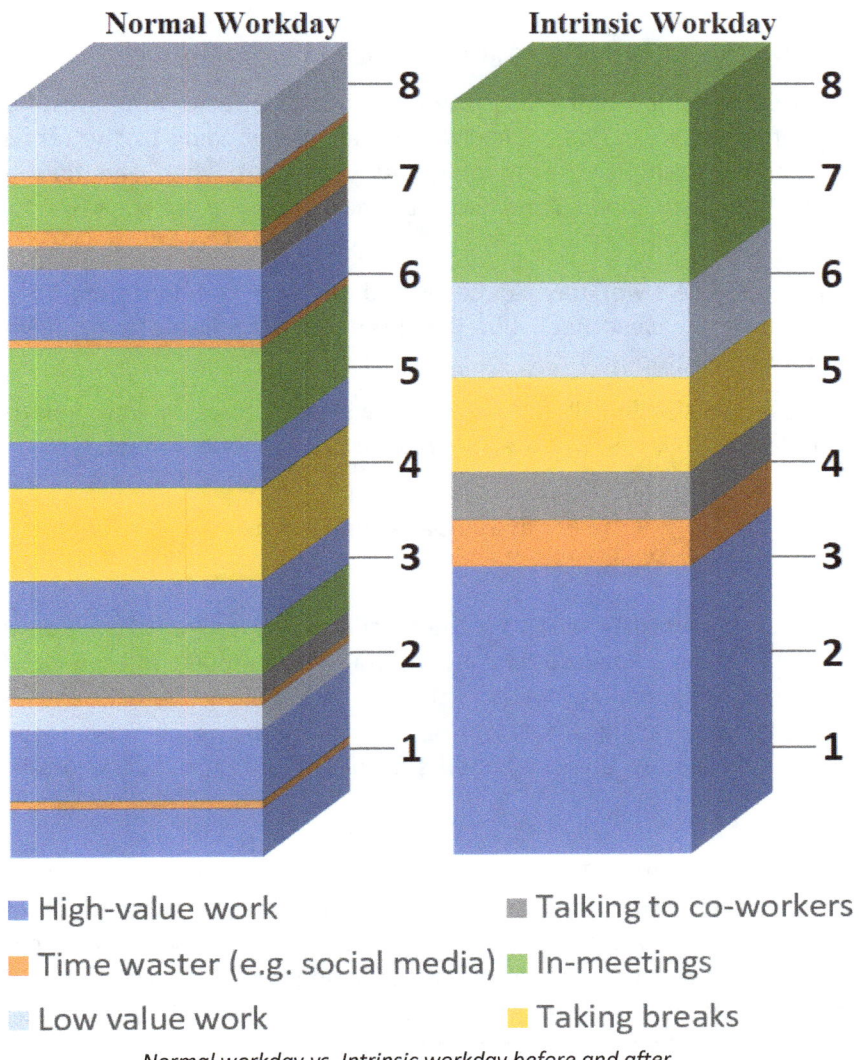

Normal workday vs. Intrinsic workday before and after

The bar graphs show my old workday verses my new workday. On the left is a colorful, but stripey mess, where I freely switched between high-value work, low-value work, time wasters such as social media and whatever popped up in front of me. If yours looks similar, that's okay, you're not alone. But it's important to realize how much time is spent dancing in and out of high-value work, on distractions, and scheduling meetings with no particular cadence. On the right, my ideal workday is shown, where I attempt to group common time habits together.

Writing an important email to your Board of Directors requires more energy and focus than drinking from and responding to the random email firehose. They both must get done, but when and how are essential distinctions. *Time habits* are not equal, nor are the tasks done within them.

Most people's workday can be slotted into four standard *time habits*. You might have others, but the intention is to frame the day in a standard method.

These one-size-fits-all chunks of time will help structure your workday. In Part 3, we'll plan the best-*levered tasks* to do within them.

Four Standard Time Habits

1. *Focused Time:* This is the most important piece of time on the planet. *Focused time* is high-brain power mode and can include designing software, writing a compelling report, or even assembling a new engine. This work draws on your deepest experience and it benefits from long-duration, distraction-free focus.

2. *Unfocused Time:* This is the work that keeps life moving. Not everything requires big-brain mode, but everything must get done. This could be filling out a business license, responding to "low-value" emails or even changing the oil in a car. Chip away at the low-value side of your work in short-duration pockets. Don't let it interrupt high-value work.

3. *Meetings:* Strive for them to be effective or reduce them to an email. Well-designed meetings are highly productive. They are a hive mind for ideas and an effective way to distribute information. However, they are extremely expensive if they are a waste of time. Not only for the wages of those present but also because it could have been productive *focused* and *unfocused time*.

4. ***Downtime:*** I have GREAT news! Quality downtime leads to greater productivity. Eat wisely, visit people, consume quality media, and most importantly: **no working during lunches and breaks**. Higher quality downtime, like a fast versus a slow phone charger, leads to greater productivity when you return to work.

Most people can fit their workday into this framework. You may have other potential work ***time habits***, but try these for starters. "Focused" work for one profession can look very different from another. The point is to be aware of time and to learn to control its structure. This is the foundation of high performance.

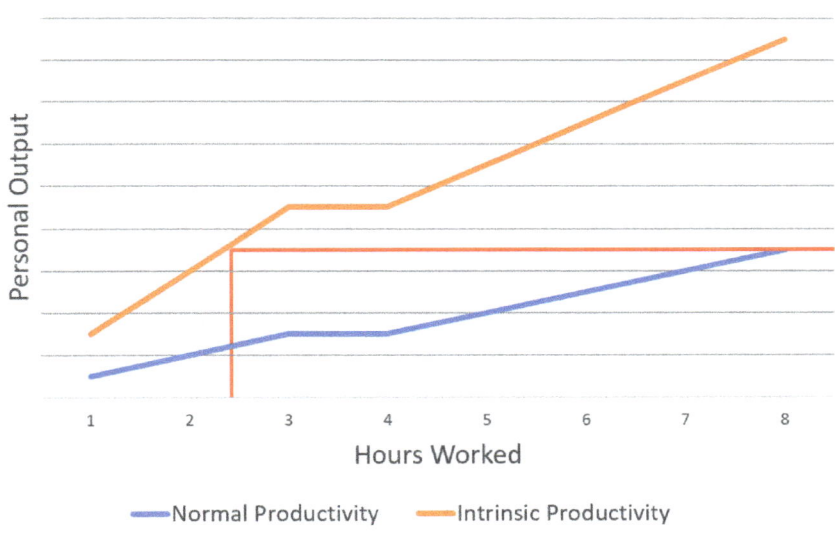

Normal v. Intrinsic personal productivity estimates

The line graph reflects my productivity with and without the Intrinsic system. In about 2.5 hours per day on average, I was able to match the 8-hour productivity found in my "normal" workday. This was calculated based on the estimated number of hours dedicated to work per week, verses hours spent in the office not on work, such as writing this book.

You can use this extra productivity however you'd like. Same hours, more output. Fewer hours, same output, or some combination. Anything is possible when work is well managed.

Remember, **time** is the most important commodity we have. Similar to wise versus poor spending habits, the results of strong time management habits are apparent over days, weeks, months, and especially years. The person who harnesses time will outperform and enjoy greater satisfaction than their peers who don't.

[4]

Focused Time:
It's Worth More than Gold

FOCUSED TIME IS the most crucial piece of the entire system. *Focused time* is big brain work. This is where you accomplish what matters most. These are the tasks that tend to be complex and benefit from deep attention. *Focused time* draws on your experience, and it benefits from being in long duration, uninterrupted blocks.

The application of *focused time* is broad. I'm writing this from the perspective of sitting at a desk. But it can be applied to anything important. Some examples of big bran focused work verses low-value unfocused work include...

Big Brain Focused Work	Low-Value Unfocused Work
Authoring a professional communication to your Board of Directors or similar audience	Scanning and responding to whatever emails arrived in your inbox
Coding a new revenue-generating component for a software platform	Responding to low-level bug requests
Assembling a new engine	Doing an oil change
Closing the books for the year	Generating a weekly status report
Selecting and implementing new software	Updating user settings
Inventing new materials in a laboratory	Ordering lab supplies

Focused time allows you to achieve more than most people within the same 40-hour workweek, or to achieve the same in well under 40 hours. Sometimes it feels like a superpower. "Work-to-Live" people shrink their work life and enjoy more free time. "Live-to-Work" people accelerate their careers by producing more, which allows them to grow into more prominent roles and/or leverage a side gig in their same 8-hour workday.

The One Thing: The Surprisingly Simple Truth About Extraordinary Results, authored by Gary Keller and Jay Papasan, suggests four continuous hours of *focused time*. I agree with this from a theoretical perspective, but it's a tough ask for two reasons:

- First, few of us can be off the grid that long.

- And second, even fewer of us are trained for it.

How to Set Boundaries for Focused Time

Our fully-connected lives expect us always to be available, answer emails immediately upon a chime, and respond to every Slack message as it pops up. This is not the path to high productivity. Most of it can wait. Rarely do we find a real emergency in these requests; people and organizations often create their own false urgencies. According to *Harvard Business Review*, in their article "5 Tactics to Combat a Culture of False Urgency at Work," these urgencies often stem from anxieties created by the individual or organizational culture.

One way to combat false urgency is by having a preference for your time and nudging your calendar and those around you toward it. I personally strive for 3 hours of continuous *focused time* every day. It fits best at the beginning of my workday before the day's chaos can push it off course. My digital calendar includes a 3-hour recurring morning meeting from 9:00 a.m. to 12:00 p.m. titled "Focused Work – Available as Needed."

At first, I only got part of it. But over time, by re-scheduling my own meetings and nudging others, my recurring uninterrupted *focused time* steadily increased, as did my productivity.

People expect responses within "learned" time cadences. Let people know about your *focused time* and that you'll respond to email and instant messages during certain hours, and that your cellphone can be used for any urgent matters. Mine rarely rings; people get it. Nudge your schedule and the behaviors of those around you.

Though today's world operates in a seemingly agile manner, stand-up meetings, on the go meetings and calls will try to pepper their way into your day. Beware of them and try to move them into your ideal meeting cluster.

Remember: Lack of planning by others is not your fire drill. And this might be hard to digest for some of you over-achievers: *Most of those emails can wait.*

If people must get feedback from you faster, try to have them batch their questions if possible. When I was an auditor, we were expected to finish all the work we were able, before asking questions. If I was stuck in one area, write down the question and move on to the next area. Once I can't go farther, then interrupt the senior person.

A friend who runs an insurance company developed a question-and-answer manual that addressed about 80% of the questions his representatives would often ask. It provided them a roadmap on how to think through the answer to many common customer questions or issues. While they could not batch questions, their number of interruptions were reduced significantly.

Finally, bosses often work at their own pace, and you might not necessarily be able to avoid that. Here is where communication is especially important. Setting boundaries with a co-worker is one thing, but doing so with a boss can be different. While I still inform them of how I work, there is a handful of people whose call I will always take and this is some of the natural give and take of the Intrinsic system. Ideal boundaries are lovely, but we can also adapt to reality.

All of us have different environments, get creative when it comes to reducing distractions from others! You know what you're striving for, identify the issues, and think about possible solutions (maybe do some research).

Training Ourselves for Focused Time

Commanding *ourselves* might be the more challenging part of achieving long-duration *focused time*. Supposing you nudged everyone else out of the way. Now you're sitting alone at your desk. It's just you and the work.

How long can you go without getting off-task?

Most of us have trained ourselves to actively destroy *focused time*. We open our big project, dive into the details, and switch to the first *ding* that pops up, and then we switch back again, *hopefully*. Regardless of outside intrusions, we often repeat the high-value, low-value dance throughout the day as shown in our graphic above.

This is where the "training yourself" part comes in. Aim for no distractions during *focused time*. You can decide how available and connected you must be.

Some helpful approaches include:

- Silence email notifications (no popups and no sounds).

- Pause messenger notifications (Slack, AIM, Teams, etc.).

- Turn cell ringer off (my phone is face up, so I usually see phone calls).

- No social media—delete notifications, shortcuts, make it difficult to use.

- No random web browsing (use an alternative browser that is work only).

- No chatting.

- No dinner planning.

- Be "off-grid," aside from what you need.

- Avoid micro breaks, keep water, and other needs stocked

- No phone or other distractions during restroom breaks

One of my favorite time wasters is posting on car related message boards. I love Pontiac Trans Ams. I could browse and post on the local area website, the big national board, and the funky homemade one (looking at you fbody.com). Over time I got to know people. So not only is there car related content, but also general banter. The cycle becomes read/post on each website, and then circle back to the first to see the response, and then read/post some more. This is an enticing time-wasting loop. I deleted their logins and links from my computer browser and I keep my phone off limits, so it's working out well.

People tell me they can never reach me. I hear their slight annoyance, but inwardly, I'm smiling. My no-distraction system is working.

Reality Check

Even with notification distractions handled, maintaining long-duration focus can still be challenging. Andy Tryba, a serial entrepreneur, wrote a training exercise on *Medium's* website. He uses an egg timer (not his phone) and ten tracking marbles. He sets the timer for 30 minutes and commits to only his planned tasks while the timer is running.

Once completed, he moves a marble to the completed side of the tray. For office workers, this helps connect our reptile brains with accomplishing something tangible. He might allow himself a brief break, then he resets for another 30 minutes and keeps going! He rarely moves all ten marbles, but striving for it produces more than he ever did before.

Photo of my desk with timer and marbles

The photo shows my setup. I keep my phone on the other side of the timer and marbles. Any impulse to check the phone is thwarted by the timer glowing back at me. Consider Tryba's method or another approach to keep you on-task during your **focused time**. If 30 minutes is too long, commit to something you *can* do. Habits start small. Intensity can always increase. It's essential to strengthen the focus muscle and grow it over time. These days I set the timer for how long I'd like to spend on the task and I try to beat it.

Multitasking is a Myth

If multitasking were real, it might look like this: Someone is reading a book while typing an email and watching a new movie. They are accomplishing a lot! Of course, there is *zero chance* that any of these are being done with quality.

Multitasking is really just juggling. You can only focus and touch one thing at a time. Excelling at important work that requires all your expertise is not compatible with juggling. During **focused time**, stick with one big brain task at a time.

Juggling harms our productivity in two ways:

- First, by being on-task, off-task, and hopefully back again, we spend less time on our most important work, and we burn extra "get back into it" time with each switch. Simply put, we reduce the number of minutes spent on the important work.

- Worse, every switch burns brain fuel. Glucose is required to motivate action. Every switch physically tires the brain, making it even harder to stay on task. If you switch to unfocused work, you burn some glucose returning to focused work. If you switch to social media, you burn a lot to get back into focused work. The bigger the distraction, especially those engineered to entertain us, the more brain fuel we burn to switch back.

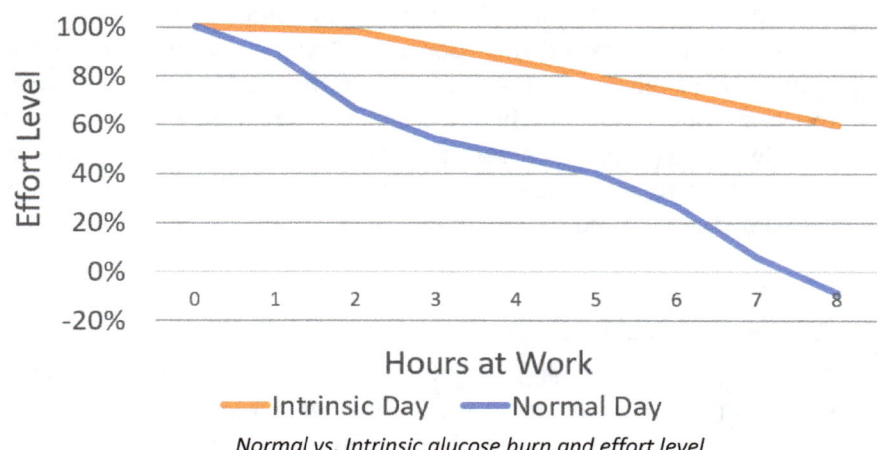

Normal vs. Intrinsic glucose burn and effort level

It's no wonder many of us are wiped out at the end of the workday. Start. Switch. Stop. Start. Switch. Stop. It's exhausting just typing that! While I didn't use a glucose monitor, the line chart was constructed based on feelings throughout the day and my ability to stay motivated and actually produce. The start-stopping, multitask days, left me exhausted and not producing much by the end of the day.

Work on one thing at a time and avoid multitasking. You'll thank me for this later.

Some professions almost require multitasking, such as a teacher grading papers while monitoring the classroom during a video presentation. In some cases, there can be a net benefit to multitasking, but this is generally the exception.

Tips for Creating a High-Focus Work Environment

Design your ideal environment for *focused time*. Ensuring you are comfortable will help with your long-duration efforts. If you work in an office, some items include:

- Ergonomic desk and chair

- Large monitor(s)

- Comfortable keyboard and mouse

- Great lighting

- Space heater; A/C unit

- Speakers or Headphones

- Storage

- Whatever else you need to make you comfortable!

I have a standing desk with an inch-thick rubber comfort mat and a stool for sitting. This allows me to keep the desk in a standing position, which promotes standing more often. I found that when the desk is lowered, I sat for more hours per day.

For lighting, I have app-controlled, adjustable smart bulbs. These are in my overhead fixture, the torch lamps behind me, and backlights behind my ultrawide monitor. This makes a comfortable "no shadow" office and a screen that is easier to stare at with the backlight behind it.

For storage, I have a bookshelf with doors and a small filing cabinet (I don't keep much paper). I also have a magnetic whiteboard and a small side desk where most desk items go.

My working environment is designed to make me comfortable for long-duration focus.

When I worked in an open concept office, it was naturally distracting with people everywhere. You'd hear chatter, people would "stop-by" randomly, so I wore headphones when trying to focus. This wasn't ideal, but neither is an open concept office! I created a long playlist of non-distracting music, like instrumental coffee shop jazz, and listened to it to cover the background noise, and make myself a little less approachable to office cruisers.

Dealing with What We Can't Control

We can't fully control our schedules but we can nudge them in a productive direction. People will schedule meetings, drop by your office, and expect responses. Unfortunately, we often operate like a stream of interruptions is a good thing.

We also have different challenges unique to us. It could be a medical issue, caring for a loved one, or any number of things that forces you to have extra interruptions in your day-to-day. That's OK.

Strive for **focused time,** and your life will begin to accommodate it. Believe me, once you start producing more in less time, you'll start finding more ways to achieve your focused time.

Action Plan for Establishing Focused Time

1. **Schedule _focused time._** Block your calendar and commit to distraction-free time. Schedule them over the next week or two. Make them recurring or re-book each week. Aim for a spot in the day where it has the best chance of happening.

2. **Inform people.** Let colleagues know you schedule **focused time** but are available as needed.

3. **Create a space for success.** Buy a big monitor, comfortable keyboard/mouse, proper desk/chair, great lighting—whatever you need to create a comfortable distraction-free space where you enjoy spending time.

4. **Train yourself.** Commit to focus and make going off-track difficult. Hide and silence your phone. If you use social media, you'll find yourself on it almost unconsciously, make it difficult to access. I highly encourage using the egg or other timed method. Also consider a second web browser for work that doesn't have fun bookmarks and logins. Make it difficult to go off task.

[5]

Unfocused Time:
Someone's Gotta Do It

THE OPPOSITE OF long-duration focus is short-duration *unfocused time*. Keep the low-value stuff that must get done, moving along without sacrificing your *focused time*. While it's still good to focus on what you're doing, not everything requires long-duration high intensity.

These tasks tend to be quicker, less complex, and can be batched together. I block recurring *focused time* in my calendar well in advance, but I only schedule *unfocused time* the day or maybe the week before. This keeps my calendar open and flexible for people who need to schedule meetings with me.

Low-Calorie Work

Not all work is equal, but most of it needs to get done. Low-calorie work fills our time but doesn't produce as much value. It usually presents itself too often, sprinkling throughout our day, causing us to switch between high-value and low-value work. Examples include:

- Reading and responding to email streams

- Responding to various messenger requests

- Checking/answering text messages

- Filling out business licenses

- Submitting expense reports

- Planning an upcoming lunch

- Perhaps dipping into your favorite time waster

Batch low-value work like this into **unfocused time** and do as much of it as possible. While **focused time** is often spent on one or maybe two major topics, we want to get as much low-value work out of the way as possible during this time.

As a reward, I might hit the car message boards for a few minutes, but that is it. I'll try not to respond to posts, to keep me from wanting to get in the read, reply, response, cycle. I'll give myself 5 to 10 minutes at the end of the unfocused time.

Still Remain Leery of Multitasking

Batching and switching from task to task is far less taxing on your brain than having them peppered throughout your day. However, even with light work, avoid working on more than one thing at a time. In Daniel Levitin's *Organized Mind*, he notes that multitasking reduces the quality of our attention. Do one specific task, finish it, and move on to the next.

In the image, James Clear demonstrates how multitasking appears busy, but produces less results.

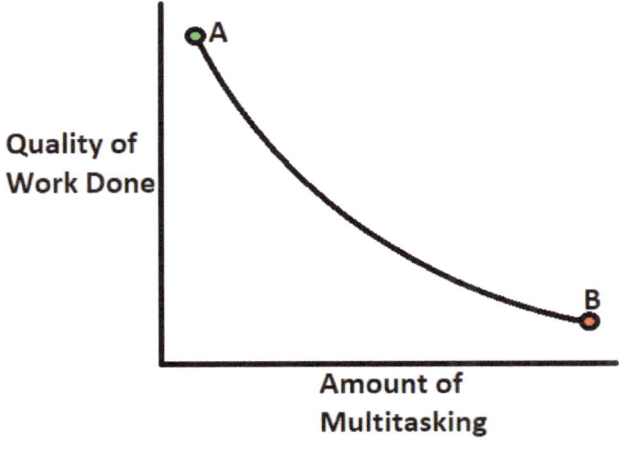

A = Looks simple, but actually gets results.
B = Looks busy, but actually wastes time.

Image credit: James Clear, *Atomic Habits*
https://jamesclear.com/multitasking-myth

Over time, you'll get better at forcing low-value work into **unfocused time**. This will naturally shrink the amount of **unfocused time** you need. The smaller this time becomes, the more time you'll have for more high-value work or extra downtime! The same can be said about meetings.

Action Plan for Establishing Unfocused Time

1. **Schedule Unfocused Time.** Block your calendar and commit to pushing through the tedious work. I usually schedule them in 30-to-60-minute increments. I re-block daily or weekly, so my schedule remains open for reality.

2. **Inform people, create a space for success and train yourself.** *Unfocused time* still benefits from many of tips associated with *focused time*.

[6]

Productive Meetings:
Use Them or Lose Them

HOW PRODUCTIVE ARE the meetings you attend regularly? Are they helpful, or are they a waste of time? Do they occur during your ideal meeting cluster or are they scattered throughout your day? The sad reality is that meetings gobble up time that could be focused, unfocused, or downtime!

The *one-hour* meeting is frequently wasted with five minutes of greeting, fifteen minutes of banter about any recent sporting events, twenty minutes of hopefully value-added conversation, ten minutes of recap and meeting minutes, and ten more minutes of socializing and/or walking back to your desk. Not to mention recalibrating your brain to get back to real productive work!

Unfortunately, this can't always be avoided. So strive to schedule meetings so they don't interrupt your ideal ***focused time.*** Don't be afraid to challenge the need for certain meetings, who must attend, and their overall effectiveness.

If we must have a meeting, it better be productive. It should have an agenda, goals, and a designated notetaker. And most of all, it should fit your ideal meeting cluster.

Schedule for Success

Ideally, cluster meetings together *outside of* your **focused time**. My ideal **focused time** is from 9:00 a.m. to 12:00 p.m., followed by an hour lunch, and then 30 minutes of **unfocused time**. Therefore, my ideal meeting cluster is 1:30 p.m. to 4:30 p.m..

I never schedule my meetings outside this window unless I absolutely must. And I request other people's meetings to occur within this window. If I'm required to take an earlier meeting, I try to make it at the beginning or the end of my **focused time**. I loathe the 10:00 a.m. meeting, but if I must take one, I try to pack them all into one day. I prefer Tuesdays.

In addition to having an ideal meeting cluster window, try to schedule them next to each other. This helps prevent time overruns. You can't be expected to stay longer at a meeting if it will make you late for your next one. This also keeps you in meeting mode. While it might not be the most fun, it results in less brain switching. It also creates the opportunity for more **focused time** if you want it.

Scheduling meetings in the most convenient part of your day is great—getting rid of them is even better!

Could this be an email?

Scrutinize meetings for necessity. As you realize the results of your **time habits**, you'll feel the *opportunity cost* of unnecessary meetings. You won't be able to shake every irrelevant meeting, but you'll shrink their footprint by remaining skeptical.

Meetings tend to come in two broad forms (and sometimes a blend):

1) **Informational**: You are mostly listening to and receiving information.

2) **Interacting**: You are part of the unique group required to further a collective goal.

Informational Meetings

Try not to let informational meetings control your schedule. If you enjoy attending and they fit your ideal meeting cluster, great. If not, try to avoid them and get the information elsewhere:

- Video replay

- Meeting deck/email update

- Discuss with co-workers

These options might not always be available, but your time is irretrievable. If you have meetings like this that disrupt your ideal schedule, consider asking for alternatives.

For example, one company would have a 9:00 a.m. all-hands meeting once a week. For participants, it is primarily informational. One person raised their hand and explained their time schedule, and management started recording the meetings, allowing employees to receive the information when it worked best for them. Guess what? Productivity increased!

If you are the person scheduling these informational meetings, consider how effective they are. Do you provide people with alternative ways to get the information? Remember, just as you should avoid *attending* unnecessary meetings, you should equally avoid *hosting* them.

Interacting Meetings

For the second type of meeting, be prepared to challenge their existence. Some meetings don't need to exist or could occur less often. You could supplement them with an email exchange update or some reporting package.

One participant had a weekly Operations and Finance meeting to address purchase order issues. Initially, the meeting created a lot of value. They made decisions on how reports would look and who would be responsible for what flags. For example, if we are beyond the expected receiving date, do the goods need to be received? Or are they late, and the expected date needs to be updated?

The value of the meeting naturally declined as they solved the broader issues. Eventually, the meetings just discussed the day-to-day, rather than dealing with major problems. This meeting was ripe to be replaced with an email reporting package. And it was.

> *ProTip*: You don't have to accept every meeting!
> Challenge the meetings on your schedule!

Are the Right People Involved?

Meetings are expensive when you add up the time of all the people involved. They are especially expensive to you as you implement and understand the cost of interrupting your *time habits*.

If the meeting is necessary, it must bring the right people together. Why are *you* and these specific people at this meeting? Is everyone the right "node" for this hive mind?

- Should it be your boss instead?

- A subordinate instead?

- Maybe nobody from your sphere needs to be there and could just be sent as information.

Who are all the others in the meeting? Ask those same questions about them. People invited can be wrong for a variety of reasons. Two common categories include:

- Lack of expertise and/or

- Lack of decision-making authority.

Managers might know less than their direct reports on technical matters (lack expertise). Conversely, direct reports might need help understanding priorities (lack of authority). People in meetings should often be swapped with someone else or not even be there.

One of our participants works for a company implementing a new Enterprise Resource Planner (ERP) called NetSuite. The ERP keeps track of everything in a business: accounting, forecasting, customers, vendors, billings, invoices, inventory, you name it. The C-Suite selected the system for purchase. Given the expense and sophistication of choosing an ERP, this makes sense from an authority perspective.

However, the C-Suite executives held on to the project during the design and implementation phase, attending all meetings instead of assigning the time to people with more technical expertise for the design phase. The C-Suite allowed themselves to be allured by nice-to-have features that resulted in an overcomplicated design. Ultimately, their ERP had to be reconfigured, delaying the project's investment return and doubling the implementation costs.

If they had thought it through and had the right people at those meetings all this could have been avoided.

When involved in a big, multi-meeting project:

- Create a meeting organization chart.

- Define who is expected at which meetings and why.

- Define a timeline to handoff the plans to the next level, as applicable.

- Review the timeline on occasion. Does this meeting have an end date?

If Meetings Must Happen, Make Them Effective

Ideally, the meetings you accept have the following going for them:

- They occur withing your preferred meeting cluster.

- They must exist (e.g., you've prodded, an email will not suffice)

- The right people are identified and you're sure it should be you.

Productive meetings accomplish their goals sooner. On a similar ERP project like the prior example:

- Bad meetings exceeded a year

- Average meetings took eight months

- Highly effective meetings took just six months.

Good meetings accomplish their mission sooner. They reached 100% earlier and, therefore, delivered value sooner. The graph shows NetSuite ERP implementations at three similar companies who had varying degrees of success. Those who ran bad meetings, took longer to implement and cost significantly more.

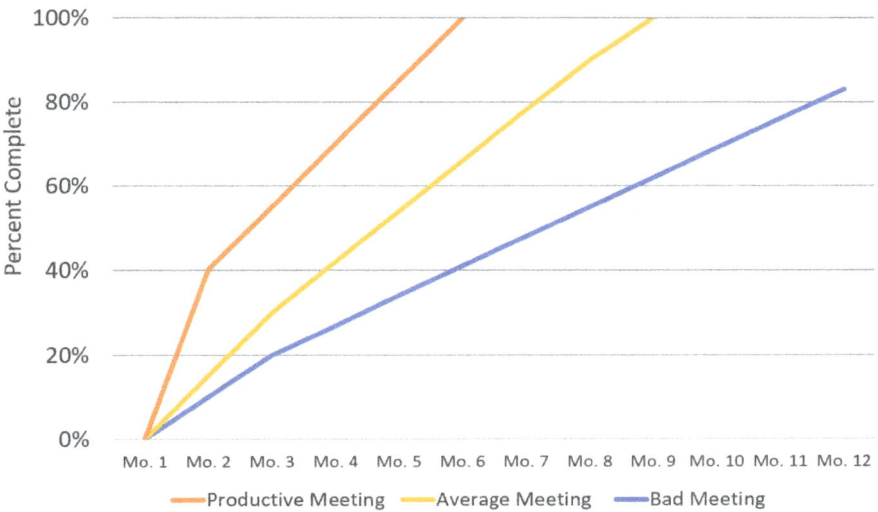

Time to completion between bad, average, and productive meetings

Productive meetings cost less, not only because they reach completion sooner, but also because they're more efficient while running. Inefficient meetings experience sprawling resource usage due to the following reasons:

- Too many people are included

- Recurs too often

- Burns an hour with nonsense, when 30min could suffice

- Does not end on time

The graph presents the average hours consumed per month during a large project. As the bad meetings fail to accomplish their mission, they often become resource tornados, increasing their bad traits as they struggle toward completion.

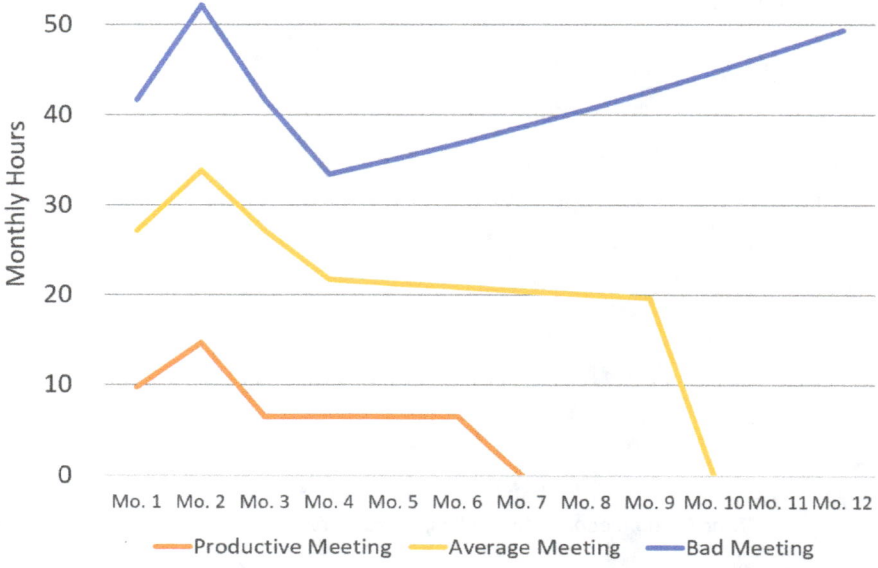

Monthly hours burned between bad, average, and productive meetings

How do we achieve productive meetings? Even back in 1976 the *Harvard Business Review* identified the benefits and drawbacks of meetings in their article "How to Run a Meeting." This timeless approach is just as accurate today as it ever was.

Productive Meetings have the following:

- Meeting goals

- Goal measurement

- Regular agenda

- Task lists with accountability: Who is responsible, for what, and when?

- Meeting org chart

Goal(s) are the purpose of the meeting. What is trying to be accomplished? It could be a one-off project like setting up a new information system or a recurring meeting, such as a sales and operations results review. Regardless of its purpose, the meeting should have a clear goal. For example:

- "Go-live with new NetSuite implementation on 12/31/XX."

- "Execute a strong sales-to-ops feedback loop to increase margin by 10% by 12/31/XX."

Large goals can be broken out into sub-goals, similar to what we'll explore in the **big goal setting** chapter.

Measurement is how progress is gauged. For a one-off project, it might be percent completion. For a recurring meeting, it might be some critical metric everyone wants to keep their eye on, such as project margin, delivery schedule, or outstanding cash receivables.

The **agenda** should be updated at the end of each meeting. Some items on it might recur, but it should include the broad topics on what will be covered next time. The point is to establish a cadence and keep the meetings focused and productive.

The **task list** should include a few very important things:

- Who needs to do what?

- What was committed to previously?

- Was it done?

- What do we expect from people at the next meeting?

Usually, these are maintained by someone performing the secretary's duty.

Review the meeting **org chart** on occasion. Ideal participants sometimes evolve as a project progresses or as skillsets change. Maybe someone needs to be added temporarily or removed and replaced. Review skillsets as the challenges evolve.

Ensure work meetings are minimalized, effective, and clustered to increase productivity. You'll produce more and work less!

Action Plan for Productive Meetings

1. **Meetings you schedule**: Scrutinize them! Can any meetings become an email or occur less frequently? If not, evaluate them for effectiveness—could they be better? Are they planned within your ideal meeting cluster? If not, move them!

2. **Meetings others schedule**: Scrutinize them! Could they be an email or other reporting package? Are you the right person to attend? Request an agenda to force the organizer to evaluate their meetings. Try to move them into your ideal meeting cluster.

3. **Before meetings**: Review your notes from the prior meetings. Ensure you've done your part. Check on any follow-ups you might need to make or materials you need to read. Come to the meeting prepared. Be engaged and be attentive. Hold others accountable for their parts.

[7]

Recharging Downtime:
Proven to Increase Performance

GREAT NEWS! DOWNTIME is proven to increase your performance. It might seem counter-intuitive, but getting away from your workspace will help you produce more. Downtime gives your brain time to process, relax, and wander.

This section aims to impress the importance of downtime and help you maximize it. Take your lunches and breaks regularly. They are important. To garner the most benefit, do a bit of planning to make your downtime high quality.

Downtime leads to Better Uptime

My old routine was the same-old grind every day. Seat time, hours, and lunch at my desk, working. Push, push, push. It was exhausting, and no matter how hard I tried or how long I worked, I wasn't getting ahead.

No more.

Now I schedule real **recharging downtime** consisting of a full lunch hour and proper breaks. My ideal lunch is 60 minutes, and breaks can be any length of time. As mentioned, I prefer lunch after **focused time** at noon and I like to have a break or two somewhere in the afternoon. It doesn't always go this way; sometimes lunch is only 30 minutes (occasionally not at all). As with all **time habits**, the more you strive for them to occur, the more often they will.

Like **unfocused time**, I schedule my **recharging downtime** a day to a week in advance. This keeps my calendar flexible leading up to the week to better accommodate real life.

Lunches and breaks are never taken at my desk. To establish boundaries and set expectations, I let people know I'm away during breaks. They can try my cell phone if they need me, though there are no guarantees.

I often remind colleagues that we're not heart surgeons (unless you are) and that immediate availability is rarely necessary. You can and should take a real break. Work-related intrusions during breaks and lunches reduce their recharging effectiveness.

Take them, and don't let them be interrupted (I have no work email notifications on my phone). Even better, find ways to maximize your downtime.

Planning for Health and Wealth

Many of us consume junk while at work. We eat unhealthy, over-priced food and spend precious time procuring it. My goal is to eat something healthy, reasonably priced, that is procured quickly. I don't want to spend too many minutes driving and waiting. Most days, I eat something pre-prepared.

Here are my usual dine-in options. For proper disclosure, I am not a nutritionist, this is what and works for me, I encourage you to research what might work best for you.

- **Pre-packed salad**: Prepared at home or bought from the store in advance.

- **Pre-packed sandwich**: Prepared at home or bought from a sandwich shop the same day.

- **Meal kit**: There are many options, such as beef and rice, chicken and orzo, etc.

- **Leftovers**: They're "free," delicious, and relatively effortless.

- **Take-out**: Somewhere fast, where you can order ahead, or delivery (though this breaks my "reasonably priced" target).

On Sunday, I'll pick up a couple of pre-made salads and stuff for sandwiches. With one leftover, my week is covered. Pre-buying also discourages take-out since you already paid for it and hopefully like it.

I also keep a stock of "relatively" healthy snacks nearby to avoid the afternoon slump. I aim for high protein, low sugar items. Not health food, not junk food. A handful of peanuts goes a long way to fending off hunger, chocolate covered ones work too!

Try to have a few healthy-ish snacks around to keep you going. This is especially helpful if your workplace has junk food onsite.

Maximize Relaxation

With good food procured quickly, you can use the remaining ~50 minutes to maximize your relaxation. Guess what that gives you? Options!

If you have a good routine where you disconnect and eat with people, that's lovely. If you work from home or generally eat alone, consider what you do during that time.

Many people eat lunch and:

- Browse social media

- Surf the internet

- Watch a show or movie

- Listen to podcasts

- Read articles

- Read books

The social media loop is always available, save it for waiting in line at the grocery store. Consider doing something during your lunch that is beyond chewing empty calories.

When I start my day I look forward to tackling my ***focused time***, and then getting lunch where I'll tune into something fun and interesting. This gives me something to look forward to during my workday, other than plain old (sometimes stressful) work.

I have a list of movies and shows I like (but my family doesn't) and occasionally watch them during lunch. I also have a few podcasts that I listen to, or I'll read a book related to my goals. The point is to plan and consume something that is *rich* to you—something that you will look forward to, so you'll be sure to take your downtime every day.

Beyond media consumption, you might also consider the following during lunch:

- No media – eat peacefully

- Eat outside

- Go for a walk or grab coffee after eating

- Anything other than working that you will personally look forward to!

There is a new trend called "silent walking," where people go on walks without their phones—no interruptions, no amateur photography, just being in the moment for a bit. In my day we called it going outside har har, but it's a great way to disconnect.

Once a week, I try to go out for lunch, by myself or with someone I want to see (this could be work-related, friends, or family). On these days, I schedule lunch for 90 to 120 minutes, giving me plenty of time to drive, park, eat, chat, and return to work.

A commitment to **recharging downtime** leads to a happier workday and increased productivity. Just the anticipation of relaxation eases the mind. The downtime itself is rewarding, but an x-factor is created by the expectation that this enjoyable time will happen. It makes the day easier as you look forward to this time coming, and the more often downtime occurs, the better the rhythm becomes.

Action Plan for Downtime

1. **Schedule downtime**: Block your calendar a day or week in advance. Commit to disconnecting during lunch and breaks.

2. **What to eat**: Regardless of what you eat, plan it. Just having it planned makes for a better lunch. Put it on your calendar or your scheduling method of choice.

3. **What to do**: Same as above. Strive for something interesting and make a list of things you can do. Avoid the social media doom scroll. Buy headphones if you need to.

4. **Dine out**: Plan something out by yourself or with company. Put the plan on your calendar.

For immediate results, plan tomorrow using the **time habits** that describe a common workday:

1. *Focused Time*

2. *Unfocused Time*

3. *Productive Meetings* and

4. Recharging Downtime

You will development a great sense of order around time, which will help you figure out how best to spend it and adjust it. Habits take about 60 days to form, so try to plan your workday by *time habit* every day over the next couple months.

Our **Super Day** app is an easy way to plan your day by time habit. Please see www.MyIntrinsicWork.com for more information. Part 4 of this book will also cover planning and doing in detail.

If you get nothing else out of this book, plan your day by *time habit*.

The results are unparalleled.

.

Part 2:
Big Goal Setting

[8]

"Why"

Identify your purpose and the best places to put effort.

THERE'S A REASON why you work and where you work. It's probably money-related and likely has some broader backstory. Maybe you love it, perhaps you hate it. Most of us live somewhere in-between.

Goals in life help us dream of what's possible. The Intrinsic stepped-approach starts by dreaming of one big goal, narrowing it into components, and dividing those into attainable annual pieces. It may sound like a lot, but it only takes a few minutes.

1. **Long-term Goal**: At the highest level (and before retiring haha), define the situation where you'd be happy or at least satisfied with work. This is your personal goal.

2. **Component Goals**: Zooming in, define up to three sub-goals that align with the *long-term goal*, for examples, a more prominent position at your current company or a new position at a different company.

3. **Annual Goals**: Zooming in further, define up to three *annual goals* that align with each component goal. For example, if you want growth at your current company, you might identify specific things to work on. Or if you want to leave, you might identify exactly what that role looks like, and steps you could take to start finding it.

Connecting your biggest dream with things you can do in the coming year will help you spot everyday opportunities that will get you there. If you returned from a walk, and I asked how many purple flowers you saw, you might recall a few. If your goal is to notice every purple flower during your walk, you'd spot a lot more of them.

Goals operate the same way. They focus your attention. Writing them down is scientifically proven to create results. Having goals and believing in them attracts success, not due to some magic, but quite the opposite.

Goals sharpen your focus. They help us ask great questions, spot opportunities, and identify what not to do. In Cal Newport's *Deep Work*, he says, "Clarity about what matters provides clarity about what does not."

Whether you know it or not, you are constantly bombarded with opportunities. Having goals in place helps you spot the good ones that apply to where you're going. They also help you avoid opportunities that probably won't get you there. (It's okay to say no!)

Goals provide purpose. This motivates us to put in the work each day that fractionally contributes to the goal. The daily work is better connected to the big picture, which provides a fantastic sense of accomplishment, knowing that what you did made some progress toward that big picture. This further motivates you the next day, which creates a motivation wheel. Goals are tangible, and re-reading them will help push you through the slumps.

Goals give us faith. It takes belief to try for your goals day-in and day-out. To achieve my goal of publishing this book, I had to have faith that it could be worthwhile, because I spent a lot of my focused time on it. Writing goals and establishing faith in them is also a circular process. Writing, believing, doing. Putting in the uncommon effort of writing goals is a "grand gesture" that will inspire your commitment.

Finally, you can share your goals with someone who cares about you to further your motivation.

Goal setting is fast, easy, and fun(ish). They can always be rewritten and will evolve. Below we discuss the types of goals, and provide case study examples that will help you quickly formulate your own goals.

[9]

Long-term Goal:
Dream Big

YOU MAY NOT know it consciously, but you have a *long-term goal* that will make you happier with work (I didn't say happy haha). I still don't know what I want to be when I grow up, but I understand how I'd like things to look: Doing work that I find challenging and interesting, while making enough money (to buy fast cars) and receiving enough time off to live my lifestyle goals (Intrinsic Life).

Your *long-term goal* should be one specific dream, related to work. It can always evolve, but the *long-term goal* should be a specific target.

Other than Retiring

If you're not ready to retire, you might as well make the best of it, whatever that means to you. Career climbing within your current lineage is a common theme for people's big *long-term goals*. In contrast, some want a better work-life balance, while others wish for change and new careers.

Depending on where you are today, there are three general long-term goal strategies:

1. **Climbing**: The primary goal is moving upward from your current position, generally along the same lineage. The reason for this goal is usually financial, prestige, etc. Upward!

2. **Mastering:** The primary goal is career stability, mastering your current or a similar position. The reason for this goal is usually work-life balance, comfort, etc.

3. **Changing:** The primary goal is changing from your current position to a different lineage. The reason for this goal is a strong desire for a change in state: wrong current career or new interests.

Your **long-term** goal should point you toward one of the three. It can and will evolve. If you want to become CEO someday, that's a *climbing* goal. When you arrive, it may develop into a *mastering* goal or even a *changing* goal as you explore something else.

We will walk through a single role as an example. Given that I was an accounting manager, it was the most obvious choice. However, at the end we provide case studies that demonstrate the entire system, in a variety of roles.

Long Term Goal Example: Accounting Manager

While this career may or may not fit with what you do, it will give you ideas about **big goal** *setting*. I selected it because it represents my day job, and it is analogous with many types of work. If you want to see more, our online database of example roles grows daily at MyIntrinsicWork.com.

The accounting managers we work with come from two general paths: Some started in private industry as general support staff, AP (accounts payable) clerks, or staff accountants who worked their way up to accounting manager. Others did the "public accounting" route, doing audits or taxes. Depending on how long they worked that ladder, they transitioned to accountant and some to accounting manager roles directly. They operated in companies of varying shapes and sizes. Our smallest represented company is a family-owned hotel, and our largest is a publicly-traded conglomerate.

The accounting manager's day-to-day consists of ensuring money transactions are processing. Accounts receivable should be sending invoices and receiving payments. Accounts payable should be doing the opposite. Expense reports should be processed in a timely manner. Overseeing this is the constant buzz is their day-to-day.

At a higher level, the accounting managers are responsible for broader financial reporting. This can include inventory, fixed asset valuations, and liability estimates, along with debt and lease accounting. They may be responsible for written policy and other technical documents. They are the point of contact in audit fieldwork. Their work ebbs and flows during the month, and many of them put in 60-hour workweeks.

The accounting managers have varying long-term goals. Some want considerable growth. Some are happy where they are. Others are looking to get into something else entirely.

Below are example goals for each type presented above:

Climbing Goal: Make CFO

Achieve chief financial officer position at a venture-backed startup, which pays $250K or better and provides ample time off.

Improving Goal: Easy Accounting

Operate in a stress-free and effortless accounting manager position where I can continue current salary (or better) while driving down hours, allowing for day-to-day personal freedom.

Changing Goal: Product Manager

Achieve a product manager position with a major shoe company. Ideally, I maintain my current salary during the switch and double it within 5 years (climbing).

This product position would have financial overlap with the accounting experience. But it would also require identifying and working trends in the fashion industry—a significant change. They also want to earn 2X their salary, so after they change, they want to climb.

These are fantastic, motivating, long-term goals. Your long-term work goal will become your North Star. Where do you see yourself in the future? Defining that goal will help you get there. Your goal will become a reference point for the broadest decisions. As shown, just a couple of sentences is enough.

Define Your Ideal Work

Think about the work you'd like to do in the biggest picture. What does this look like? Any number of **big goals** can be crafted for one's work, aim high with yours!

Goal levels can be **doable**, **stretch**, or **possibility**. Aim outside your comfort zone. Aim for what might be possible.

Long-term goals don't have a time element. It might be nice to put "within three years" at the end, but that's not the point. Consider this goal "lifetime big." Don't constrain it with time. It doesn't have to be perfect, and it will evolve (I still don't know what I want to be when I grow up).

[10]

Component Goals:
Dream Specific

BREAK THE BIG *long-term goal* into a few pieces. This makes it easier to think about. My work *component goals* include:

1. Success at current company

2. Success at a new company (finding that just right "goldilocks" role)

3. Success in a new field (leverage experience to kickstart a new career direction)

You might have others, but these are a good starting point for most people. Our examples will focus on the first *component goal*. Improving your current work provides immediate benefits with no tradeoff cost (switching jobs isn't fun and is not always the best answer). This component goal will encourage and help you find opportunities where you're at. Even if you don't think they exist, it's worth looking for them while you're there.

Once upon a time, I left a company where there were many opportunities. They had recently turned over upper management, and I felt like I was left alone on an island. Rather than waiting for the new management to come around or even attempting to force my role toward what I wanted it to be, I found a new job. That new job sucked, the prior company's stock options would have been worth millions. Closely consider internal options before you leave.

If you create a goal for **success at a new company**, get into the weeds on defining what that new company looks like. Not only your specific role but also what the management looks like, who the investors are (if applicable), what kind of culture the place has, and ideally, you will have an interest in their product.

And when you think you've found it, make sure it is real. I joined a company that told me they were going to the moon. The financial forecasts turned out to be inflated and they got rid of a ton of people including me shortly after I joined. That really sucked.

If you create a goal for **success in a new field**, get into the weeds looking for overlaps with your current experience. It's easier to switch if there is some obvious overlap you can use as a steppingstone. A corporate finance professional who was considering a switch into sales leveraged their finance experience by selling corporate finance software first. They had instant credibility with their corporate customers, and now with successful sales experience they can transition into selling whatever they want in a next role.

We deep-dive into all the work-related goals in Intrinsic Life. Based on the examples here, you should be able to write your own component goals beyond **success at current company**. As with all of our goals, these are the stock examples designed to fit most people; you may have others.

Let's take a look at this goal more closely.

Define Success at Your Current Company

Think about your current work. What could you achieve there that might help your long-term goal? If your current role isn't an obvious fit with your long-term work goal, give it more thought. Look around your organization for what might fit. You'd be surprised what opportunities exist when looking through the "goals" lens.

Component Goal Example: Accounting Manager

Returning to our example role, our accounting manager looked around their organization for what might fit. As a reminder, their **long-term goals** are shown below:

- Climbing goal: Make CFO
- Mastering goal: Easy Accounting
- Changing goal: Product Manager

When considering their current companies, the accounting managers come from various businesses. Some are at monster companies, where there are ten of their roles. They report to regional controllers, who report to a corporate controller. That person might even have a layer or two between them and the CFO.

On the smallest end, some work for small businesses, reporting directly to the owner. Most are somewhere in the middle, often managing a team of 3-5 people while reporting to the controller, who reports to the CFO.

They have varying **component goals** related to **success at current company**.

Climbing Goal
Work with the corporate controller on new responsibilities that expand the experience of the accounting manager. Delegate some existing work down to inspired staff accountants. Ideally, I work my role toward Sr. Accounting Manager or Assistant Controller and increase earnings by 25% or better.

Improving Goal
Hone the monthly close and audit reporting. Both take way too long and are very painful. The goal is to shorten my average workday by 50%.

Since our office only notices when you show up, I'd like to use this free time to work out in the middle of the day.

Changing Goal

Work cross-functionally with the design team on a project with the goal of creating some resume material. Discuss with head of design, on what they look for on a resume, for a mid-level product role.

You now have a **big long-term goal** and a **component goal** narrowed to your current work. Next, we'll zoom in to a manageable time horizon by breaking the **component goal** into three **annual goals**.

Annual Goals:
Dream Attainable

LONG-TERM, NORTH-Star-level goals are great. But they must connect with reality. The last step is to break your **component goal** into granular annual pieces. This helps you dissect your goal, which increases your chances of making progress toward the **long-term goal**.

Divide your annual goals into three barely achievable pieces. The more challenging they are, the more creative you'll need to be to solve them. The accounting manager who wants a 3-day financial close will look at things very differently than the one who wants a 1-day close. Challenge yourself.

Don't worry about getting your annual goals wrong; it's easy to re-think them and re-organize them. My **component goal** and **annual goals** often alter and influence each other and tend to evolve every few months. While they can overlap with formal workplace goals, they can be something different entirely. These are *your* goals and you can write and update them accordingly.

These near-term goals will become the basis for our **levered task planning**.

Define Your Current Company Annual Goals

Think about the **component goal** you wrote for **success at current company**. What could you do in the next twelve months to make traction toward that goal? If your current role isn't an obvious fit with your long-term work goal, get creative.

Depending on their **component goals**, we found the following **annual goals** related to **success at current company**. As a reminder, we aim to create around three **annual goals**—*climbing, improving, and changing*.

Annual Goal Example: Accounting Manager

When considering their upcoming year, accounting managers have an assortment of possible things they might do to further their goals within their existing workplace.

Climbing Annual Goals related to making CFO

1. **Cash Forecasting**:
   Get involved in the company's cash forecasting process; ideally, improve accuracy and reduce time to create the reporting package.

2. **1-Day Financial Close**:
   Prove functional excellence by improving accounting close processes and NetSuite utilization.

3. **Improve Margin**:
   Work cross-functionally on *Product Budgets* and *Sales Contracts* to help improve deal economics.

Improving Annual Goals related to easy accounting

1. **Ease Reporting**:
   Ease monthly reporting by improving processes and system utilization.

2. **Smooth Audits:**
   Work with auditors to establish materiality and identify issues before field work.

3. **Uplevel Team:**
   Delegate annoying parts of my role; expense report approval and close calendar review.

Changing Annual Goals related to product management

1. **Product Team Collaboration:**
   Engage with our Product team. Better understand what they do and, ideally, work on projects together.

2. **Learn Margin Story:**
   Review prior product pitches to understand the sales story (compare with actuals that you can pull from the accounting system).

Don't be afraid to envision the future in your downtime

Consider your goals when thinking about your downtime and media consumption. For example, I want to become a CFO someday and heard about a book I had to read. *The Outsiders* follows the careers of extraordinary leaders, those who achieved extraordinary results in comparison to their peers.

It was introduced by the highly influential "Secret CFO," an online persona for an unnamed Fortune 500 CFO. The lingo and up-leveled thinking the book provided helped me secure a VP level finance position, one more step toward CFO.

Action Plan for Big Goal Setting

Define your goals:

- One long-term goal

- Up to three component goals

- Up to three annual goals for each component

If you don't have a big-picture goal or even a component goal, work it backward.

Define up to three **_annual goals_** to attempt this year. Turn that into a **_component goal_**. Write the **_long-term goal_** when you figure it out.

As mentioned, these will evolve. Their primary function is to help establish your purpose. Their secondary function is to establish your priority.

For **_big goal setting_** worksheets, see MyIntrinsicWork.com.

Part 3: Levered Task Planning

[12]

"What"

<u>Strategies to make progress on big goals!</u>

WHAT YOU DO in any given moment is your productivity. Two people with the same base abilities attempting the same goal will experience wildly different outcomes based on the quality of their tasks. By planning your tasks, your efforts will produce more, and your mind will appreciate the plan living outside your brain. You'll be able to detach easier in your off hours, while accomplishing more.

This chapter connects your recurring work *time habits* (focused, unfocused, meetings, and downtime) with your annual goals to build the framework for *levered task* planning. These tasks are the granular steps that push the goals along. They instruct you on what to do in the moment to bring about success. Accomplishing them is very satisfying, because you can see their connection to your *long-term goal*.

Starting with *annual goal #1*, consider what you can do during *focused time* to move it forward. These are the tasks where you lock out the world and dedicate your energy and knowledge toward the work. Next, consider what you can do during *unfocused time*, *meetings*, and *downtime*, either recurring or one-off. These tasks might be things you already do or new work you'll find.

Designing High Quality Tasks

Everyone has their own method for tracking tasks. Keeping lists (paper or spreadsheet), adding them to calendars, various applications, and other methods. We'll get into list making tips in our Helpful Tools chapter. This section is about designing high-quality tasks. The table below presents our framework in grid form. Considering the ***annual goal***, what tasks could be done within the given ***time habits***?

Levered Tasks		Time Habits			
		Focused Time	**Unfocused Time**	**Meetings**	**Downtime**
Annual Goals	**Cash Forecasting**	Task #1 Task #2 Task #3...	Task #1 Task #2...	Helpful meeting(s)?	Media? People?
	1-Day Financial Close	Task #1 Task #2 Task #3...	Task #1 Task #2...	Helpful meeting(s)?	Media? People?
	Improve Margin	Task #1 Task #2 Task #3...	Task #1 Task #2...	Helpful meeting(s)?	Media? People?

Planning tasks helps in a few ways. It gives you a plan of action of what to do in the moment without burning time figuring out what to do. It's like giving yourself instructions or a workplan for your day. Writing out the steps also helps free your mind from thinking about work after hours. Once you've written the outline, it's out of your head, all you must do is put it in motion when the *time habit* is available. Perhaps the best reason for writing out your tasks is that you'll continually improve them.

My goal for *Intrinsic Work* is a book and an application. I had the steps written for launching the companion application well before it would ever go into motion. But it's out there, even though I didn't have the priority (or capacity) to address it yet. By having it as a written goal, my thoughts about how to launch the application evolved. I started to notice new bits of information that have helped my learning and thinking about apps. As a result, having a detailed plan allows your approach to improve before you even start working on it. By the time I created the app, the approach and my planned tasks was so much better than my original plan.

[13]

Uplevel Tasks with Research

OTHER PEOPLE HAVE likely attempted similar goals and projects, so start with some research. Research helps us identify the best tasks we can do to achieve our goals. In practice, I oscillate between research, doing, learning, and repeating. This often increases the ceiling of my written goals.

Learning and practicing leads to mastery, which leads to better questions and bigger answers (the tasks you could do).

Other People Have Done This Before

Research is looking for the best approach. Study the success of high achievers and learn from the failed attempts of others. There is value in both, and learning from the mistakes of others is far less painful than learning from your own.

Beware of your "natural approach" when attempting challenges. Depending on familiarity, most people are presented with a problem and give it their best shot. They have a solid ***annual goal***, consider what they know, and dive in. This might be good enough for some things, but not where it matters most.

The One Thing: The Surprisingly Simple Truth About Extraordinary Results, authored by Gary Keller and Jay Papasan, suggests that research allows you to move from E to P.

- From (E)ntrepreneurial and crafty to

- To (P)urposeful and methodical

Moving from E to P is about finding the best approach. Or at least something better than what you would have conjured up naturally. This results in using your time with greater purpose. This will make you more productive with your efforts, allowing you to produce more or work less.

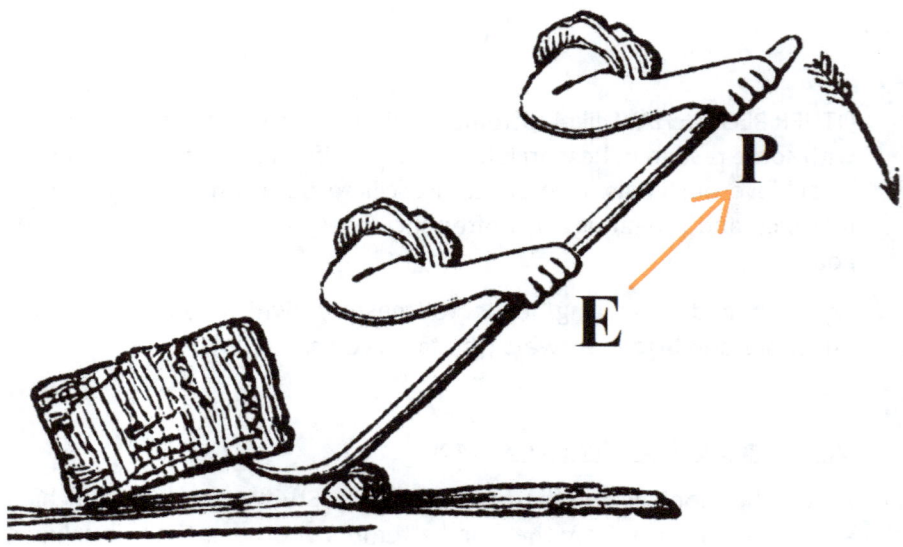

Leverage your actions by doing "P Level" work
https://experihub.com/what-are-the-different-kinds-of-levers/lever-clipart-14/

If you're spending time on a task, it's much better to be pushing from the levered position. There are many ways to research and become more purposeful, including online searches, articles, message boards, B2B offerings, books, and discussions with colleagues and mentors. Look for ways to level-up your approach and shortcut goal achievement.

Even if you are often a strong producer, there still might be a better way. Statistically speaking, you're probably not the most intelligent person on the topic. Challenge your natural approach and ceiling. Look for new models/systems, brainstorm ideas, and seek out BIGGER ANSWERS to your POSSIBILITY LEVEL goals.

When I Inherited a botched NetSuite install, that could hardly process transactions, I started by crying, and then did some research. A lot of it. This lead to me finding a "User Acceptance Testing" template that helped me think, plan, and strategize much better than I could using my natural approach.

Research and *doing* are meant to complement each other. Along the way, you'll learn and advance. This will result in more complex goals, which will create more complex questions—questions that will require new research and bigger answers. Your natural approach and ceiling will expand along the way.

80/20: Lean in Where it Matters Most

In addition to finding the best way, the 80/20 principle suggests that 80% or more of an outcome is determined by 20% or less of the effort. This principle is true in many aspects of life, especially at work.

Our accounting manager who wants a one-day close, benefited by identifying the "long pole" items in the accounting close process and addressing those first. These are the tasks that took the most time and effort. In this case, how their Oracle accounting software handled deferred-revenue transactions made the accounting close for revenue take 5-6 business days, their longest item.

By researching online, they found other companies with similar issues and a few elegant solutions. By changing internal processes and working with the business systems team, they were able to harness worldwide revenue transactions into the 1-day close. Solving the most complex task first immediately freed department resources. These people went on to solve the next items, which created a resource-freeing snowball in just a few months.

Prioritize your tasks to achieve early payoffs wherever possible, and realize the benefits sooner. *One hundred percent* of the effort is still required to achieve the goal, but the 80/20 approach helps us to identify and complete the pieces that produce the most significant gains *first*. Lean in where it moves progress the furthest, the fastest, and enjoy earlier returns.

[14]

Goals + Time = Task Planning

WITH *TIME HABITS* identified, **big goals set**, and a method for up-leveling tasks, it's time to plan your *levered tasks* in granularity. Tasks can be one-off or recurring. They are bite-sized, actionable pieces of your goals that can be completed and checked off daily.

Zooming in on the climbing goal, we layer our *time habits* and *levered task* questions for each **annual goal**…

Accounting manager

- ○ **Make CFO**

  - ▪ **Success at Current Company: Annual Goals:**

    - • **Cash Forecasting**

    - • **1-Day Financial Close**

    - • **Improve Margin**

      - ○ What big brain tasks could be done during *focused time*?

      - ○ What small, but needed tasks could be done during *unfocused time*?

      - ○ What *productive meetings* could help achieve this goal?

      - ○ What can be done during *recharging downtime* to help the goal? People to dine with, books to read, etc.

These layers are the basis for designing and planning your tasks.

Granular Planning: A Place for Everything

The format you use to identify and track all your tasks is up to you. We'll introduce various real-world methods in Part 4, for now we'll deep-dive into the ***levered tasks*** identified by our accounting manager doing the climbing goal.

Levered Tasks Example: Accounting Manager

Accounting managers fit the Intrinsic framework obviously when considering the nature of their workday and tasks.

Focused time is used for deep work. Tasks that benefit from long-duration focus. Developing new policies, designing better systems, and reconsidering role designs (who does what, when). Many aspects of their work responsibilities fit here.

Unfocused time is used to tackle the little stuff. Reviewing weekly internal controls reports. Checking emails and responding to Slack messages (or their corporate interruption tool of choice), and all the other little stuff.

Downtime promotes productivity. Accounting managers often eat at their desks and need to break the bad habit. They can plan some productivity beyond media consumption as well, including lunch with staff, peers, boss, and others.

Meetings tend to occupy a significant amount of the accounting manager's time. *One-to-ones* with direct reports, regular meetings with department heads, and meetings with various functional bosses. Vendor calls, customer calls, and ERP meetings. They stack up.

Consider what tasks fit best within those *time habits*. They can be adjusted over time. The point is to think about and plan at a very granular, actionable level. Lets have a closer look.

Climbing Goal: Make CFO: Success at Current Company: Cash Forecasting: Time/Tasks:

Focused Time:

1. Research corporate cash management best practices; update plan/tasks.

2. Cash out: design purchase order report/template to use with operations organization to better plan inventory related payables.

3. Cash in: design a sales order report/template to use with sales organization to better plan receivables.

4. Cash out: design operating expense report/template to use with the broader organization to better plan expenditures.

5. Bring the above together into an executive reporting package.

Unfocused Time:

1. Each Monday, create and distribute the weekly management reporting package.

2. Read blogs, such as the Secret CFO for inspiration.

Downtime:

1. Monthly – Lunch with the operations department.

2. Monthly – Lunch with the sales department.

3. Quarterly – Lunch with other department heads.

4. Consider listening to a finance podcast.

Meetings:

1. Meet with operations weekly to review status.

2. Meet with sales weekly to review status.

3. Meet with "other major spenders" monthly to review status.

Eventually, delegate these meetings.

This is a brief example. Consider your *annual goals*, the *time habits* you have available, and write out the tasks you can do in the moment. For your task list to be useful, all your tasks must be on it. After considering all the tasks that fit your *annual goals*, identify everything else that is your responsibility and their ideal *time habit*. Store and assign yourself tasks in whatever format works for you. Remember, your goals and tasks will evolve, it's okay if they're not perfect. We want them out of our heads where they can evolve.

Look to Delegate

When thinking about tasks, consider what you can delegate. If you manage people, delegate work that will give your people upward experience and/or give them the stuff you don't like doing (sorry). If you're not a people manager, still consider what others could do. Some tasks might be better suited for others in your department or someone else entirely. Voicing a compelling case can shift work.

One of our **accounting managers** reviews the staff accountant's bank reconciliation files each month. This proved to be interesting the first few times, but it got a little old after a year. As such, this task no longer had alignment with any annual goals. This accounting manager also has "senior accountants," one of which wants to become an accounting manager. The staff accountant's reconciliation review was delegated to this person, creating a win-win situation. The accounting manager no longer has to do it, while the senior accountant gains supervisory experience.

An **office manager** had an IT-related task that was annoying and clearly did not fit any of their annual goals. The task was adding and removing people from the Human Resources platform. While this sounds easy enough, steps in the process often required research and phone calls. When you get down to it, this office manager is not an HR professional, and the "easy" HR platform was, predictably, not easy. It was their least favorite task.

While this person had no one to delegate the work to, during focused time they researched how to run the platform better and figured out a solution. The COO sends all offers and fields all responses. As such, headcount-related transactions originate solely with this person. The office manager proposed that the COO work with a part-time virtual resource they found. This person would cost a tenth of the office manager's salary, is an HR specialist, and comes with significant experience with the company's HR platform. The COO thought it was a no-brainer and approved it on the spot.

In the book *Deep Work*, Cal Newport suggests considering what aspects of your work could be transferred to a newly-graduated college student and over what period of time. If you could hand a task off in a week or two, the task is probably not leveraging your experience and is ready for delegation.

After mapping all your responsibilities, consider what you'll do, and where others can help. It is okay to let go of things. Design quality procedures, teach people how to perform the steps, and hand them off!

Look for Automation

"But we've always done it this way."

A phrase I've heard more times than I'd care to admit. Depending on your role, automation or other process improvement opportunities might be obvious, challenging, or impossible. Some things can only be sped up so much.

- An accounting manager wanting a 1-day close can continuously look for ways to squeeze the processes. The transactions ended yesterday; they just need to speed up data collection and compilation (not easy, but they do it).

- A construction supervisor can find ways to speed up job site builds, but they can only go so fast before quality declines. Further, there is a physical speed limit; even if quality could be maintained, drywall and framing can only go up so fast.

Real-World Example:

The accounting team had a few issues that made it difficult to know the revenue number on day one.

First, the sales department would enter their completed sales orders whenever they wanted. This made it difficult to understand what was immediately sold.

Next, the Oracle ERP was set up in a way where knowing revenue versus deferred revenue (that's where the company got money but did not complete service) required a complicated spreadsheet. This sheet pained the auditors and required several layers of internal review during its week-long preparation process.

These short-comings combined made revenue reporting the longest item in the accounting close.

Real-World Solution:

The solution on the sales side was twofold:

First, the accounting manager lobbied the CFO for a policy change. The sales department is now required to have completed sales orders entered by the last day of the month. Additionally, commissions would no longer be backdated and would be based solely on the date the sale order was entered (a strong accountability mechanism).

On the systems side, the accounting manager found an Oracle module that was relatively inexpensive and replaced the scary spreadsheet. After a few meetings with the business systems manager, the add-on was approved and implemented the following month.

Between these two changes, revenue could be accurately estimated on day one, and they moved on to the next daunting item: their 25-year warranty reserve estimate!

Challenge your tasks for automation. Are there things you do, that could shrink or disappear completely?

After mapping all your tasks and sending some for delegation (hopefully), your task list is complete. Pat yourself on the back! This is a huge step!

Your task list will evolve; it's never perfect, but you now have a roadmap. Writing goals-to-tasks forces you to think about the most granular things you can do to succeed.

Next, we'll explore how to bring about action day-to-day and over the long haul, where it really matters, where the real results are made.

Action Plan for Levered Task Planning

1. Write out ALL your work tasks by **annual goal** + **time habit**. This can be in your format or by using our application at MyIntrinsicWork.com (we'll review these next).

2. Consider any "Other" tasks that don't fit nearly in your goals. It is important that ALL TASKS are on your list. This frees your mind from having to remember anything.

3. Identify items to delete: Delegate or Automate.

Part 4: Drive Momentum

[15]

"How"

Run the system with ease and free your mind after hours.

DEFINING *TIME HABITS*, writing **big goals**, and identifying **levered tasks** puts you well ahead of most people. Unfortunately, design and strategy are the easy parts. Implementing and sticking with your plans is the hard part. This part will help you "stick with it" day-to-day and over the long haul, where the big results are made.

Driving momentum involves daily planning, accountability methods, and helpful tools that propel day-to-day production.

The aim is to make your highly-impactful productivity effortless (or at least easier). You can have a high-functioning work life where you produce more while working less hours. Use it however you want, achieve more at work or achieve more with your passions outside of work, perhaps some combination.

Humans are creatures of habit. The better we introduce rhythm and the ability to predict our time, the better we use it. Habits and routines allow us to execute easier without relying on our own finite willpower to stay on task. Techniques to perpetuate momentum include:

- *Daily planning*: Map the day by **time habit** and assign yourself *levered tasks* to do within them.

- *Accountability methods*: First establish accountability with yourself, it is surprisingly powerful. Uplevel by including trusted partners who will champion your efforts.

- *Helpful tools:* Here we introduce trusted systems, which are organizational techniques for keeping track of everything. We also introduce motivating psychology, which includes concepts (and further reading materials) on how to free your mind from work-related stresses.

The success of our goals is pushed through our daily habits and habits make doing the work easier, if not automatic. Accountability methods and helpful tools aid their perpetuation.

[16]

Daily Planning:
Real World Time Management

PLANNING YOUR DAY promotes productivity and is extremely freeing. Here, we create a snapshot of the next workday by *time habit* and *levered task*. This helps us in two significant ways:

1. Well planned = Being more productive in the moment. Just follow your instructions. You're not wasting time figuring out what to do.

2. Well planned = Less reason to think about work after hours. You're roadmap is planned, there is less reason to think about it.

Super Day: The Intuitive Planner

For our *daily planning*, we first map our day at a high level by *time habit* in consideration of our real-life schedule and responsibilities, to create a doable plan each day. From there, we prioritize the tasks we'll attempt during those times. Planning this way allows you to visualize the time you have. It also allows you to see how effectively your time is presently slotted.

This exercise can be done analog or digital, whichever you prefer. I like planning my **Super Day** using the Intrinsic Work application available on MyIntrinsicWork.com. I print mine to a physical copy to give myself an itinerary to look at and scribble notes on. Conversely, some people use the template in PDF or just put everything on their digital calendar. We'll explore techniques in the Helpful Tools chapter.

When I first started trying to schedule my day by **time habit**, it made the fragmentation obvious. My schedule had the **time habits** willy-nilly scattered throughout the day, as shown:

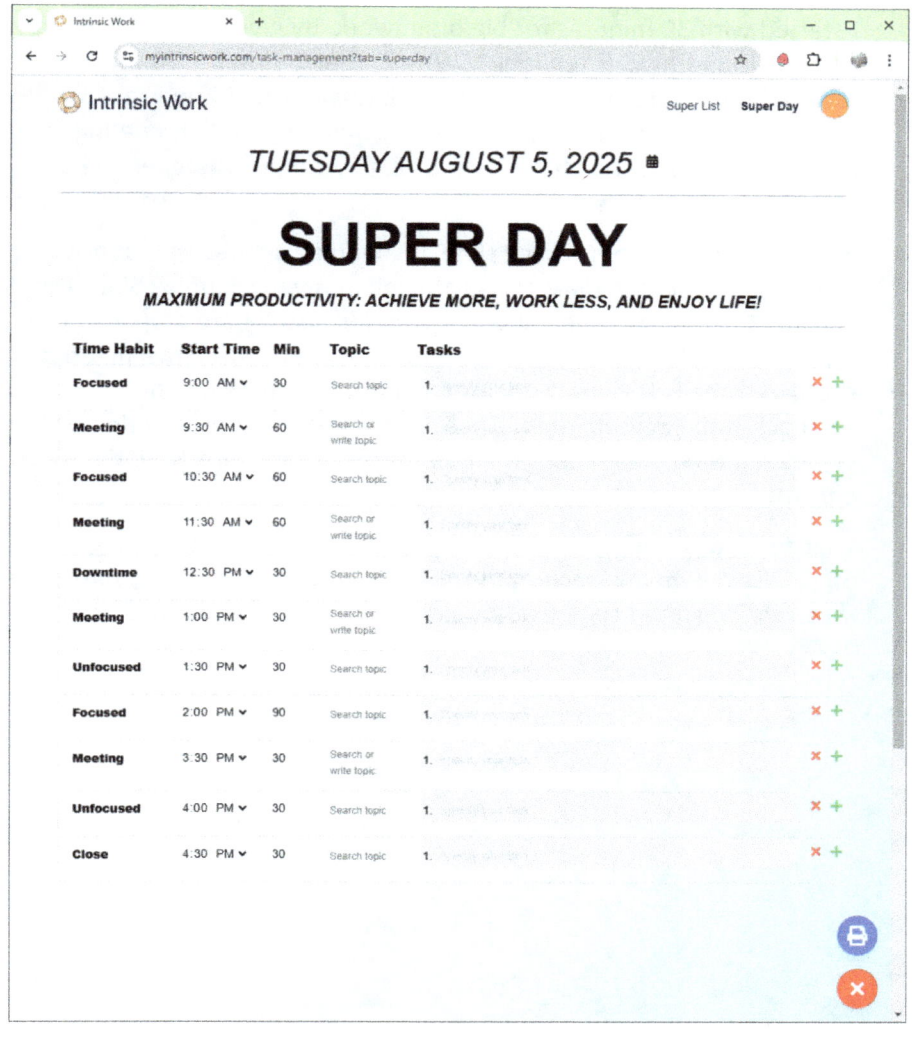

A Super Day planner as it appears in the app, available at MyIntrinsicWork.com.

I started with 30 minutes for big brain work. By giving the *time habit* a name, I found myself realizing, "Why bother trying for 30 minutes of *focused time*?" Because right off the bat, whatever important work I was focused on was interrupted by some meeting. At that meeting, new information would reach me and probably derail whatever the good plan was just yesterday.

After another hour of *focused time*, I scheduled a meeting that not only broke up my *focused time*, it also ate half of my lunch hour! Since there is a meeting on the other side of lunch, it's also a hard stop, so I can't run late, which makes lunch even more rushed. After the meeting, I shuffled some low-value work during *unfocused time* and hopefully, I'd get back into *focused time*. Then there was another meeting, more *unfocused time*, and finally, the *daily close* (a new *time habit* discussed below).

That same day nudged into my ideal schedule would have a big chunk of *focused time*, a *recharging lunch*, *unfocused time*, *productive meetings* clustered together, and then the *daily close* as shown:

Monday August 5, 2024

SUPER DAY

MAXIMUM PRODUCTIVITY ON MASSIVE GOALS, EVERY DAY!

TIME HABIT	START TIME	GOALS AND TASKS	Do it?
Focused Time	9:00 AM		[ ]
Lunch	12:00 PM		[ ]
Unfocused Time	1:00 PM		[ ]
Meeting #1	2:00 PM		[ ]
Meeting #2	3:00 PM		[ ]
Meeting #3	4:00 PM		[ ]
Meeting #4	4:30 PM		[ ]
Close	5:00 PM		[ ]
			[ ]
			[ ]

This provides a long lean in time and a solid lunch with no hard stop, since I've scheduled **unfocused time** after lunch. It doesn't matter if I start on the email firehose at 1:00 p.m. sharp or 1:04 p.m. After 1:30 p.m. is when I prefer to start taking meetings.

Meetings are lumped back-to-back-to-back-to-back together. This isn't particularly fun, but it's very effective. It keeps you in "meeting mode." Engaged, taking notes, and attentive to the purpose. It also forces meetings to end on time.

Comparing the days, the ideal day has *time habits* tightly grouped together, while the fragmented day moves in and out of them without concern:

TIME HABITS	Ideal Day	Normal Day	TIME SPENT
Focused Time:	**1 occurrence**	3 occurrences	180 minutes
Unfocused Time:	1 occurrence	3 occurrences	60 minutes
Meetings:	Back-to-back	Scattered	180 minutes
Habit Switches:	**4 switches**	**10 switches**	**420 minutes**

The ideal day has one long focused time and fewer switches

Three hours of regular, uninterrupted *focused time* will allow you to accomplish whatever you want, while fewer switches result in easier execution. You'll produce more while enjoying an easier workday. It's a win-win.

After years of nudging my schedule, something this perfect shows up on occasion. After lunch, it is usually more chaotic. One meeting owner has put a weekly 9:00 a.m. recurring on my calendar, and random ad hoc stuff still sprinkles its way in.

If a meeting must interrupt your ideal *focused time*, push it toward the poles. For my schedule, 9:00 a.m. at the beginning or 11:00 a.m. toward the end is best. Maybe 11:30 a.m., and push or shorten lunch. The 10:00 a.m. meeting in the middle is the worst. There are days when I'm unable to schedule *focused time*. And that's okay. This system is flexible, and the next day will likely be better.

As you shape your calendar, try scheduling recurring slots of *focused time* where it makes sense for you. If your mornings are full of meetings or other demands, perhaps *focused time* is best suited for the afternoon. It can also be any length of time that works for you, the point is to rope off part of your workday to big-brain work.

No matter how ugly and scattered your current schedule, viewing it through the *time habits* lens will help you improve its structure and the *levered tasks* you accomplish.

Super Day: Plan your Tasks

You have your day mapped by *time habit*, now review and prioritize what *levered tasks* you'll plan for tomorrow during those times. Assign yourself a reasonable but aggressive workload for the next day. The more robust your *levered task* list, the better you can prioritize what matters most.

Assigning yourself *levered tasks* can be done in whatever way works for you. Depending on how you create and store tasks influences the process. People who keep their tasks on paper might assign themselves prioritization for the next day with a simple red pen numbering system. The spreadsheet crowd, re-numbers and sorts their tasks for the next day; some print their task list, while others refer to it digitally. The Intrinsic app includes the *Super List* which stores tasks by time habit and goal. These flow into the *Super Day* as options when planning. However you operate, give each of your *time habits* a clear task assignment.

Returning to our accounting manager example, along with glimpses into a couple of other roles, we present an ideal day for each person. It includes possible tasks related to their *climbing goals*. The accounting manager's ideal day is the same as mine—*focused time* in the morning, lunch, *unfocused time*, meetings, and then the *daily close*.

Monday August 5, 2024

SUPER DAY

MAXIMUM PRODUCTIVITY ON MASSIVE GOALS, EVERY DAY!

TIME HABIT	START TIME	GOALS AND TASKS	Do It?
Focused Time	9:00 AM	1.Research Financial Reporting Best Practices; Update Plan/Tasks Below 2.Review close calendar; consider what can be	[ ]
Lunch	12:00 PM	Trader Joe Salad - Listen to CFO Thought Leader podcast	[ ]
Unfocused Time	1:00 PM	1. Check emails - respond to quick ones 2. Check Slacks 3. Run Open PO Report - send to Ops	[ ]
Meeting #1	2:00 PM	Meeting with banker to discuss parking our investment money in government treasuries	[ ]
Meeting #2	3:00 PM	Weekly 1:1 with Boss - update on Close Project status	[ ]
Meeting #3	4:00 PM	Monthly meeting to discuss the Close project	[ ]
Meeting #4	4:30 PM	Weekly Operations Meeting - Discuss flags from PO report	[ ]
Close	5:00 PM	1. Squash Desk Notes; do 2-minute tasks 2. Update Task List; Checkoff Weekly Plan 3. Plan tomorrow's Super Day and Tasks	[ ]

Office managers tend to have a different look. They often have busy work and meetings in the mornings. As such, many of them schedule meetings and unfocused time early and aim for a *focused time* somewhere in the afternoon:

Monday August 5, 2024

SUPER DAY

MAXIMUM PRODUCTIVITY ON MASSIVE GOALS, EVERY DAY!

TIME HABIT	START TIME	GOALS AND TASKS	Do it?
Meeting #1	8:00 AM	Daily Planning Meeting	[ ]
Unfocused Time	9:00 AM	1. Check emails - respond to quick ones 2. Check Slacks 3. Attend to fires	[ ]
Meeting #2	10:00 AM	Daily Site Meeting	[ ]
Unfocused Time	10:30 AM	1. Check emails - respond to quick ones 2. Check Slacks 3. Attend to fires 4. Read Safety articles.	[ ]
Lunch	11:30 AM	Order before leaving, pickup tacos. Listen to WorkSAFE podcast on the way, and during lunch.	[ ]
Unfocused Time	12:30 PM	1. Check emails - respond to quick ones 2. Check Slacks 3. Attend to fires 4. Read Safety articles.	[ ]
Focused Time	1:00 PM	1. Redline current safety policy	[ ]
Unfocused Time	3:30 PM	1. Final email/slack/fires	[ ]
Close	4:00 PM	1. Squash Desk Notes; do 2-minute tasks 2. Update Task List; Checkoff Weekly Plan 3. Plan tomorrow's Super Day and Tasks	[ ]

Construction supervisors have different days and are often forced to be more fragmented. They arrive early in the morning to get the workers going. Afterwards, their managers want status and update meetings. They're the first at the scene if something goes wrong on the ground. They take lunch relatively early in the day. Afterwards, they take care of paperwork, ordering materials, worker issues, etc., until it's time to go home. Our creative construction supervisor chopped their *focused time* into two ninety-minute parts:

Monday August 5, 2024

SUPER DAY

MAXIMUM PRODUCTIVITY ON MASSIVE GOALS, EVERY DAY!

TIME HABIT	START TIME	GOALS AND TASKS	Do it?
Meeting #1	7:00 AM	1. Review the plan and build goal for the day 2. Safety and Quality reminder 3. Review yesterday's work	[ ]
Meeting #2	8:00 AM	Daily meeting with Ops Manager - discuss yesterday's progress	[ ]
Unfocused Time	9:00 AM	1. Check and respond to emails 2. Take phone calls	[ ]
Lunch	10:00 AM	Home made sandwich - read Construction Project Management book	[ ]
Focused Time	11:00 AM	Download site P&L report over time and for different jobs. Study trends. Compare with what you knew working on the job	[ ]
Unfocused Time	12:30 PM	1. Take Calls 2. Respond to Fires 3. Run current weekly report, identify trends.	[ ]
Focused Time	1:30 PM	Continue studying historical P&L reports.	[ ]
Close	3:00 PM	1. Squash any Notes; do 2-minute tasks 2. Update Task List; Checkoff Weekly Plan 3. Plan tomorrow's Super Day and Tasks	[ ]

Consider your real-life responsibilities, schedule your *time habits* where they fit, and prioritize meaningful *levered tasks*.

Recall the approach for *focused time* and *unfocused time*. During *focused time*, aim for zero distractions, in a comfortable setting, and focus on that high-value, big brain work. During *unfocused time*, push along all those little tasks and get the low-value work out of the way. Always keep in mind that *perfection is contrary to productivity*. Identify the best way to complete your tasks and see them through to completion.

Remember: Contributions to an outcome ARE NOT evenly distributed. All work is NOT created equal. Prioritize tasks and devote time where it matters most.

ProTip: Only schedule tasks that can be reasonably achieved in the allotted timeframe. If there's no room for **focused time** on the **Super Day**, there's no point attempting tasks that require focus. Be aggressive, but also be realistic and kind to yourself. The whole point is to make your work life easier, not harder.

Daily Close: Ease Your Mind

The **daily close** helps you sleep at night. This **time habit** is your end-of-day cleanup and **Super Day** planning time. It's essentially more **unfocused time**, but it's far too important and therefore receives its own **time habit** callout.

The **daily close** should be slotted at the end of the day when productivity is done, and all new information has been received. This is the time to plan the next day with renewed prioritization:

1. Harvest email and notes

2. Do small tasks

3. Update your **levered task** list

4. Plan tomorrow's **Super Day**

Harvest Email and Notes

My email and notes generally contain of one or more of the following:

- Tasks

- Information

- Nonsense (haha)

Tasks

Tasks can be found in the various requests that reach our inbox, or were jotted down as notes during a meeting. Get the quick ones out of the way in the moment, while putting others on your task list.

- Small tasks: if they can be done in a few minutes, do them now.

- Remaining tasks: all others go on to your **levered task** list to be prioritized and addressed later.

Information

Information is something that might be helpful someday. It could be a note taken during a meeting or something mentioned in an email. It could be thoughts about a system design or a comment about a potential new training program. All my information goes into my electronic notes organizer, discussed below.

Nonsense

Nonsense still might go in the notes organizer. If it's on paper, I toss it in my "maybe recycle" stack, while others go straight in the bin. I don't organize my email at all. All of them just sink to the bottom after harvesting for tasks and information. Worst case, the search feature can always recall them later, but important ones usually make their way back to the top on their own if I missed something.

Update the Task List

After harvesting emails and notes for tasks and information, update your **task list**. What did you accomplish during the day? Scratch out completed items and update the next steps as necessary.

Plan tomorrow's Super Day

Guess what? After updating your task list, your "work data" is now reset. Planning tomorrow can commence:

1.   Map the Super Day by time habit.

2.   Prioritize the levered tasks you'll attempt.

3.   Plan your recharging lunch.

4.   Print your Super Day!

You are ready for the next day!

Make the Daily Close a Priority

Make the **Daily Close** the last item before leaving work when possible. This is helpful for two reasons:

- It's when you have the most information, as mentioned above, your work data is now reset and you're less likely to receive new emails or meeting requests.

- Most importantly, it becomes your mind's signal that the workday has ended, which will help you better enjoy the off-hours.

Having the **most information** is obvious. The later in the day, the less likely new information or new calendar invites will show up. This is the point in the day when you have the most information for planning and prioritizing your effort for tomorrow.

Declaring an end to your workday is less obvious. This "ritual" tells your mind it's time to let go. It becomes the recurring signal to your brain that the work day is over!

And here is the difficult news: it must be over.

No evening email checks, no mental replays of conversations, no scheming about upcoming challenges. Shut down work-thinking *completely*.

According to Cal Newport's *Deep Work*, even short dashes into work-related activities fracture relaxation. Like switching between tasks, switching between work and non-work taxes your mind. You might not be "relaxing" after work, but making dinner and responding to low-value work emails is rarely a winning combination.

Rest is better achieved with unbroken relaxation, save the low-value work for **unfocused time**. Each time relaxation is broken, you slow down and even reverse the restful charging speed. Arrows in the graphic indicate when I dipped into work after hours, and the percentages are based on my feelings and next-day productivity.

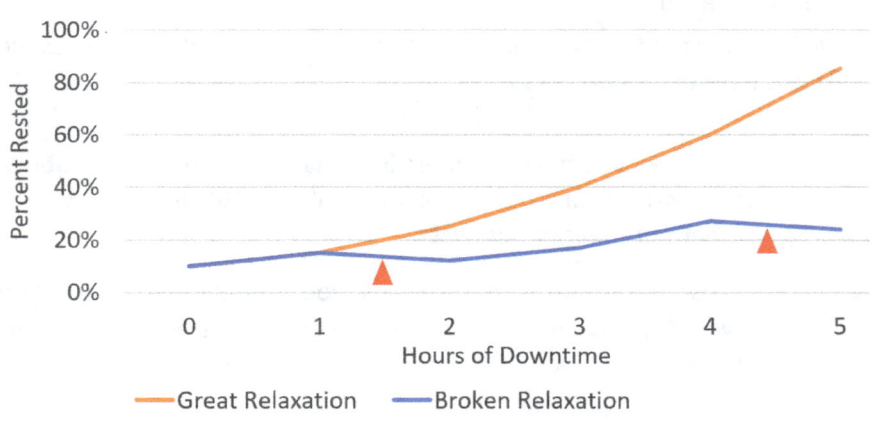

Broken verses great relaxation during your downtime

The worst part is these taxing interruptions rarely produce high-value productivity. They tend to align with unfocused work at best. Sometimes they resolve themselves by other people who live attached to their low-value work overnight. Leave work, at work. You are free! This also gets easier as your working hours become more productive; you simply have less reason to check on work.

Action Plan for Levered Daily Planning

1. Plan your **Super Day** for tomorrow. Map out **time habits** and plan your **levered tasks**.

2. Commit to leaving the work at work. Outside of special projects (and I mean really special), or some emergency, we don't produce much value during this time.

3. Repeat daily. Remember it takes about 60 days to form a new habit, so keep this going for a couple months.

[17]

Accountability Methods

YOU MAY HAVE chased goals in the past and missed the mark. We all have; it's hard out there. Staying with it and keeping motivated is challenging. This section is designed to help you stick with it and get through the hard parts. This will help you to keep going over the long haul, so you can enjoy the reward you deserve, be it increased output and/or working less.

The better you manage your time and tasks daily, the stronger your cadence will become. Habits need about sixty days to form, but nudging your schedule has an indefinite timeline. Therefore, don't get discouraged if things don't always go as planned. Just be sure to pick it up the next day and keep trying.

The best way to keep going is with accountability.

Be Accountable to Yourself

Start by committing to a goal and tracking results with just yourself, it motivates progress. In the business world, they say, "Measure what matters." Each Friday I plan generally, what I hope to accomplish the following week. As with everything in the Intrinsic system, you can do this in whatever method works for you, but its good to have a way to checkoff and measure. One level up from the **Super Day** is the **Super Week**. This helps you plan and then reflect on the week.

Super Week: Track Your Performance

Momentum builds momentum. The **Super Week** helps you keep a plan and scoreboard around your **time habits**. Toward the end of the week, review your calendar and make a general plan for each time habit.

My usual goal is five occurrences of **focused time** per week, though I'll reduce that amount if there's something in the way, such as an all-day meeting (or hopefully a vacation). When I first started it didn't always go well, but as I've nudged myself and those around me, it's gotten better.

When building new habits, just showing up is a win! My weekly goal tracking is simple: Yes or No on whether I did them. I'm not concerned with when in the day, or the number of minutes, just Yes or No on whether I showed up. You can track minutes or other metrics, but simpler is easier to start. The Super Week is available within our app at MyIntrinsicWork.com.

TIME HABITS WORKWEEK							
TIME BLOCK	DESCRIPTION	Goal (days)	MON AUG 28	TUE AUG 29	WED AUG 30	THR AUG 31	FRI SEP 1
FOCUSED	Free from all distractions, focus on this Work only.	_ out of 5	Yes No	Yes No	Yes No	Yes No	Yes No
UNFOCUSED	Chip Away at this Helpful Work	_ out of 5	Yes No	Yes No	Yes No	Yes No	None
MEETINGS	Recurring Help and Accountability	_ out of 5	Yes No	Yes No	Yes No	Yes No	None
LUNCH/ BREAKS	Disconnected Breaks Increase Performance	_ out of 5	Yes No	Yes No	Yes No	Yes No	Yes No
Goal Tracking	Finish CPE to CPA License	150 min	0	60	60	30	0

Super Day planner. You can also write in the high-level topics you hope to cover.

Beyond *time habits,* you can incorporate other goals into the weekly planner. Suppose you need to dedicate 150 minutes weekly of Continuing Professional Education over the next five weeks to keep your CPA license active (I always wait until the last minute). You could map a plan for those minutes and strive to achieve that weekly target along with everything else. Beyond work you could track a reading goal, a fitness goal, and anything in your life that could use some measurement—all in one place.

If you adopt a weekly planning method like this, marking the *Super Week's* daily progress becomes the 5th step when planning tomorrow's *Super Day*. This allows you to reflect on the plan and compare it with the day's results.

Initially my Super Week hung in my office, but I eventually moved it to the refrigerator so others could see my progress. This helped my recurring weekly successes by creating low-pressure accountability with people in my house who walked by it.

Uplevel with an Accountability Partner

Even stronger than committing to yourself is having an *accountability partner*. This is someone who is on your side and, ideally, someone who can offer feedback and guidance. These people are immensely helpful in keeping you on track and up-leveling your approach.

The goal of a work-related accountability partner is to provide extra motivation to keep you on task. This should be someone you enjoy interacting with—a person who is interested and will cheer you on during wins and losses.

Having someone to discuss your plans with, at any level of detail, will help you keep those plans. Even better, discussion adds a new perspective and will influence the quality of your goals and tasks. The relationship will expand your potential.

When making decisions, it can help to stratify, to assign categories. I consider there to be four different types of work-related accountability partners:

- **Peer**: this is someone at the same level as you. For example, you both are accounting managers, or perhaps one is a marketing manager. You both are in the same general level.

- **Friend**: for this purpose, it should be someone who can relate to the goals you're after. An accounting manager aspiring to be a CFO would probably have better overlap (for this purpose) with a friend growing a construction company, than a friend who is a docent at an art gallery.

- **Mentor**: the better aligned they are with your trajectory, the bigger the benefit. For this example, for the accounting manager, a former CFO or CEO would be a terrific mentor. Other executive disciplines or other leadership positions would also be helpful.

- **Mentee**: similar to the mentor, but opposite. Mentoring someone coming up your lineage is probably the most helpful to everyone. But anyone trying to build their career could benefit from chatting with you. While they might not have as much world experience as a mentor, they can still help keep you on track, and they might add a viewpoint that you never expected.

You can choose the level of detail you share with this person:

- Time Habit Goals (and how calendar nudging is going)

- Work Long-term Goal

- Work Component Goals

- Work Annual Goals

- Work Project/Tasks

You can be formal or informal with how and what you share. With my senior-level mentor, we discuss things at a higher level. Long-range goals, accomplishments, and trajectory. We discuss these things, but don't have anything formally written down. With my peer accountability partner, we're both using Intrinsic, so we have plans written down, and discuss what we're up in a lot of detail. We get into the weeds around the tasks we planned and how time planning is going. Ideally, you talk with an accountability partner weekly.

To find your accountability partner, brainstorm a list of possibilities. These could come from your mind, or by reviewing connections on LinkedIn, Facebook, or other platforms. Look for people you like but never talk to. Build a list of maybes. Even if they don't line up perfectly with your work, anyone is better than no one.

Whittle the list subjectively—gut reaction, career alignment, or any other method you choose. I categorized my list of possible partners in Excel. I assigned them as peer, friend, mentor, or mentee and arbitrarily scored them 1, 2, or 3. I ended up with a handful of people in each. Ultimately, I picked a Peer:1 and a Mentor:1. I Reached out to them with a very straightforward message:

Hi Peer:1,

I want to catch up with people I like but never talk to. Would you like to do a Zoom or lunch one of these days?

Here is my calendar link: https://app.calendarbridge.com/book/jSAX9lj

Best,

Andrew

This is easy and people are very receptive to people from the past popping up to say hello. They both responded, and I went on to contact others. I reached out to a former CFO through LinkedIn and started having occasional Zoom calls with him. It wasn't regular enough to be an accountability partner, but he still gave some great advice and introduced me to new opportunities. Some people I have recurring weekly meetings, while others who have my booking link, just show up on my calendar occasionally, which is awesome.

One of our accounting managers sought out an audit manager (peer) who they worked with at an accounting firm. Another contacted a CFO (mentor) who worked at a prior company. Both did this on LinkedIn with a simple hello message. They now meet with these people regularly, which has opened new opportunities for both of them.

Action Plan for Accountability

1. Plan the week by ***time habit*** and track your progress. The Super Week template can be found at

    MyIntrinsicWork.com.

2. Consider adding other measurements helpful to your life.

3. Brainstorm possible accountability partners. This should be someone you'd like to spend time with.

4. Reach out to a few of them and see where it goes.

[18]

Helpful Tools:
Make it Easier

YOU MAY HAVE noticed that many common tools are seamlessly incorporated into our system. You probably use many of them already.

Our **trusted systems** section describes where all your work data can go. This helps you stay organized and frees your mind from trying to remember everything.

The **motivating psychology** section helps you identify things that help you perform better and those that derail progress.

This section will help you develop effortless organization while keeping your mind motivated, which boosts your productivity potential and frees your mind afterhours.

Trusted Systems: A place for everything.

Humans are not designed for the stream of information and complexity that bombards our brains in modern society.

There's too much of it. And it's constantly advancing.

I used to waste time looking at several calendars just to make an appointment. I would look over a handful of task lists to figure out what to do tomorrow. My notes were everywhere and all this just makes doing the work slower and a lot more painful. The better I got leveraging tools and technologies, the easier all the became.

People harness their life-data very differently. Those who are good at organizing the onslaught of data are naturally more effective. Once running well, an organized life-data system provides a recurring benefit that is practically free. This also leads to greater productivity and/or working less.

Our **trusted systems** include:

- Calendar
- Lists
- Notes
- Supporting systems (to harness specific complexities)

Trusted systems can be digital, analog, or hybrid. From sophisticated pieces of software to simple pieces of paper. Whatever works for you!

The point is to have a well-designed system for your life's information. Using it will make your life easier and free your poor brain from trying to remember every little thing.

Your reliance and the resulting benefit only come if you trust the systems. Incorporate tools that you are likely to use and stick with.

Have Your Calendar Work for You

The most common trusted system already used by most people to some degree, is the calendar. Digital or paper, the effectiveness of calendar usage varies tremendously.

Upcoming appointments: Do they live exclusively on one calendar? Or do you need to reference other sources to get a complete look?

- Personal calendar

- Work calendar

- Other calendars

- The refrigerator

- Memory (oh no)

The better you can see what will command your time, the better you'll manage it. I recommend putting all time commitments on one calendar. Your **Super Days** are easier to plan, and are more successful with fewer surprises "popping up". Better, putting all commitments in one spot eases your mind from trying to remember them.

The key is using the calendar on a regular basis. This means everything needs to go on it, and it means reviewing it regularly, so you'll trust that you'll see your time commitments coming. While stating the obvious, if you fill out a paper calendar and never look at it, the system won't work.

Review your calendar daily and scan out a few weeks to see what's coming. You can set reminders minutes, hours, days, weeks, and months in advance on digital calendars. On paper calendars, you can always write a reminder before the date. The point is to have good visibility into what's coming. During review, I'll sometimes identify things I need to add to my tasks list to prepare.

For those with multiple calendars, combine them. If you use paper, transcribe them all into one spot. For those with numerous digital calendars, consider a tie-together application. At one point I had four work-related digital calendars, which was a nightmare to manage.

After trying several apps, I found CalendarBridge to be very effective (see MyInstrinsicWork.com for discounts). Now, everything cross-books automatically as busy, while my personal calendar receives the full details from all the other calendars. This puts everything in one place which makes planning easy, it also includes the booking link builder that can be sent to people.

> *ProTip:* Use your calendar. Put everything in one place. Reference it often. Remember, there is nothing more important than time.

Lists to Free Your Mind

Are the tasks you need to get done written somewhere or are they in your head? Most of us have lists, and they tend to be dreadful, okay, or excellent. As you can imagine, those on the latter end of the spectrum naturally get more done with less effort, they are simply better organized, and can easily prioritize the highest value work.

How you keep track of your *levered tasks* associated with your *big goals* might be the most critical list you keep. They come in many forms: paper lists, spreadsheets, fancy applications, and many other methods, including the Intrinsic Work application.

Regardless of your preferred format, *list design* and *usage* are extremely important.

Usage, like the calendar section, means every task goes on the list. It also means referencing it regularly and doing the tasks that are on the list. Stating the obvious again, you can't put tasks on a list and then just forget about them.

For **design**, great lists have the following:

- Prioritization

- Custom Enrichment

Prioritization for a task list can come from due dates, a numbering scheme, or any method that helps prioritize your daily work. Even just reviewing and selecting based on feelings, the point is to consider your tasks and identify what is best to work on the next day.

One analog approach we identified is the 3" x 5" indexing system. Each 3" x 5" card is one or a group of tasks which you prioritize based on deck order. As you complete them, they can be torn up, which is a wonderful feeling of accomplishment.

For a people list, prioritization can come from birthdays (think adding a column), a last met with date, or just reviewing it and contacting people on occasion.

Custom enrichment is where the list has room to assign more attributes and give more meaning to the data. For example, the Intrinsic task list is unique, and allows you to assign tasks their best *time habit* and *big goals*.

A people list can be enriched by asking if the person is a possible *accountability partner*, with selections for Peer, Friend, Mentor, Mentee or N/A. If you do this, they don't have to be contacted right away, but having an easy reference list makes it easier. You could also customize a people list, questioning whether to invite them to your Summer BBQ? Yes, No or Maybe.

There are many ways to store tasks. From a grid format, as previously presented, to a possible spreadsheet format shown here:

Component Goal	Annual Goal	Time Habit	Tasks	Due Date (optional)
Success at Current Compar	Cash Forecasting	Focused Time	1. Research Corporate C	
Success at Current Compar	Cash Forecasting	Focused Time	2. Cash out: Design Purd	8/5/2025
Success at Current Compar	Cash Forecasting	Focused Time	3. Cash in: Design Sales	
Success at Current Compar	Cash Forecasting	Focused Time	4. Cash out: Design Ope	
Success at Current Compar	Cash Forecasting	Unfocused Time	1. Weekly - run reports, u	
Success at Current Compar	Cash Forecasting	Unfocused Time	2. Continue researching	
Success at Current Compar	Cash Forecasting	Unfocused Time	3. Email - check and resp	

Spreadsheet method for tracking tasks by goal and time

I've mentioned the people list. While having a task list is obvious, most of us don't have a people list. You know a lot of them, but most of us could manage the relationships better. They live in our social media, and we like their posts, but that is not engaging in the relationship in any meaningful way.

I built my people list by sourcing names from social media, corporate org charts, along with some critical vendors and customers. You only have to do this once, and then just maintain it. On my list, I added a custom enrichment to track by relationship type, friend, family, professional or other.

Relationship	Person	Next B-Day (optional)	Accountability Partner?
Friend	Bill Rogers		No
Friend	Sara Smith		Peer
Family	Mabel Martinez	4/15/2024	No
Family	Hank Kim		No
Profesional	Jennifer Grant		Mentor
Profesional	Bernie Ramirez	12/10/1980	Peer
Profesional	Wendy Jones		No

Spreadsheet method for people

Whatever fashion you keep your lists, try to make them flexible. I'm an accountant, so I naturally love spreadsheets. They're easy to work with, and adding a new column for enrichment is easy. If I'm hosting a party, I can add a column for "Invite to New Year Party?" to quickly draft a Yes/No/Maybe guest list. Please see our People List within the Intrinsic Work app.

Quasi-list Items

Say you need to contact your tax accountant in 8 months. You can keep this on your task list toward the bottom, or you can put a reminder on your calendar around that date. This keeps your list smaller, and when the date comes, you can push the reminder, send the email, or move it to your task list.

Organized Notes

Lists are designed to hold items of information about something specific. Notes are more general, but their design and usage are still important.

Like the prior sections, usage means putting all your notes in one place and reviewing as needed. You must use your notes and trust that you'll continue to do so. You can't put notes in one place, and another, and another.

The format for your notes can be digital, analog, or hybrid. I use a monster running Word doc for ALL my notes and utilize the navigation pane and the "styles" to create nested categories. I type almost all my notes into this document, I even wrote this book in the same format, shown below. By having the stratification built, it makes it very easy to drop new information into the best spot.

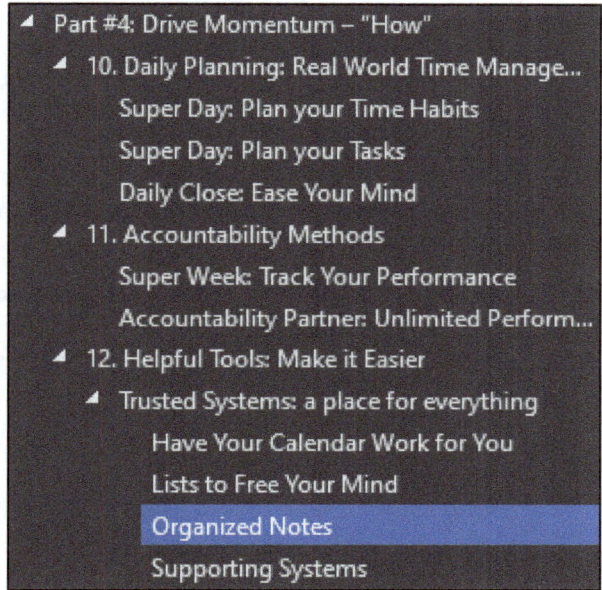

Intrinsic Work organized navigation pane

For work notes, the same stratification as your tasks can be used. They can also be designed around certain events, such as notes related to a specific recurring meeting or a large project.

If you keep paper notes, slot them into pre-labeled folders or some organization method. I keep both digital and paper. Usually, I type important stuff into the digital file and less important stays on paper and lives in my paper organizer. I review it monthly to consider digitizing or tossing.

I glance through my notes once a month to mine for information. I'll delete stuff or move it around, and sometimes it gives me a new idea that generates a new task, and on the task list it goes!

One of our construction supervisors uses a basic paper filer, divided into a few recurring topics, such as safety, budget, and personnel. The foreman requested information from the last meeting, and the construction supervisor pulled up the information in seconds. That person demonstrated their strong organization on the spot.

Store your notes however works best for you, but they should be organized around a system and maintained regularly.

Supporting Systems

Calendars, lists, and notes are great standard systems that most people can utilize for higher performance. However, sometimes we need a location for more complex work.

For example, I often have customized Excel workbooks for specific projects. While helping a company raise their Series A, I had an Excel workbook that served as my one-stop for everything fundraising-related. This included:

- Margin Plan

- Manufacturing Costs

- People and Contractors

- Equipment

- Operating Expenses

- Financial Overview

- Task List

- Organized Notes

This workbook became a topic-specific trusted system. In addition to the stratification of topics above, the workbook itself contained many sub-levels. Margin broke out into sales and costs, and those broke down into specific granular pieces. This framework made it easy to incorporate new information and to track good questions.

It also captured both tasks and notes, which significantly reduced the complexity of my task list and notes files. Rather than including all the tasks related to finishing the Series A raise, the task list is simplified to "Continue the Series A workbook, see tasks therein."

Similarly, working on a technical document can lead to a supporting system. One of our office managers drafted a Plant Operations Manual. This technical document has its own strata of varying chapters, sections, and sub-sections. By writing out the strata first, and adding a task/notes section, the document becomes a supporting system. A one-stop for everything on the topic while it's being worked on.

During an operations meeting, the office manager heard about a preventable accident and wrote it into their notes. During their **daily close**, they jotted the incident into the safety section of their technical document, rather than their general notes. Eventually, they'll reach that section during **focused time** and can incorporate the example into the overall document however they want.

An emerging type of Supporting System is artificial intelligence or AI. There are seemingly endless AI options out there, such as OpenAI's Chat GPT, Google's Gemini (formerly Bard), and many many others. I don't have a strong preference, they are all "large language models" which operate in similar fashions. They can produce text, graphics, videos, software code, all sorts of things, based written prompts. They can also summarize large volumes of data by feeding them files.

I used one of them to write the following paragraphs on AI options and the risks of using AI. Its very easy.

Prompt #1: You are authoring a self-help book. In it there is a section on artificial intelligence tools that might help people be more productive. Please write a paragraph on AI tools the reader might consider.

This produced a pretty good paragraph, but I wanted more.

Prompt #2: Please add specific AI tools by name the user can try.

Prompt #3: Please add risks of using these tools

Here is the result:

As technology continues to evolve, artificial intelligence (AI) is emerging as a powerful tool to enhance productivity. Consider exploring AI-powered tools like virtual assistants such as Siri, Google Assistant, or Alexa. These assistants can schedule meetings, respond to emails, and even summarize lengthy documents. For those struggling with writer's block, AI-driven writing assistants like Grammarly or Jasper.ai can offer suggestions, improve grammar, and even generate content ideas. By harnessing the potential of these AI tools, you can streamline your workflow, reduce stress, and achieve your goals more effectively.

I really liked that last part about goals. That summary is pretty good, here's what it said about the risks of AI:

While AI-powered tools can significantly enhance productivity, it's essential to be aware of the potential risks involved. Data privacy is a major concern, as these tools often require access to personal information. Ensure that the tools you choose have robust security measures to protect your data. Additionally, overreliance on AI can lead to a decline in critical thinking skills. It's crucial to use these tools as complements, not replacements, for human judgment and decision-making. Finally, bias can be present in AI algorithms, leading to unfair or discriminatory outcomes. Be mindful of the potential biases and ensure that the tools you use are designed to mitigate them. By carefully considering these risks and using AI tools responsibly, you can harness their benefits while minimizing potential drawbacks.

It's not terribly surprising that the AI summary ended the risk section about itself in a positive tone.

Trusted systems come in many forms and allow organization to come naturally. Everything related to Work ends up in one of a few places:

- Calendar
- Task List or People List
- Notes File
- Supporting System

David Allen, who authored *Getting Things Done: the Art of Stress-free Productivity*, suggests getting as much out of your mind and into your system as possible. Allen describes the achievement as having a mind like water. The mind is clear and not bothered by trying to hold on to everything.

Harnessing information will shave hours off your workweek, leading to greater productivity (or working less).

Action Plan to Get Organized

1. Define the one master calendar you'll rely on and cross-book everything to that calendar.
2. Define how you'll keep your task list and people list—populate both.
3. Define how you'll store notes.
4. Consider any supporting systems you can deploy.

Motivating Psychology

Getting all our work data out of our brains and into a **trusted system** is fantastic. This section includes a few tidbits of motivating psychology to make productivity even easier.

The techniques in this section have made it all easier if not enjoyable. I used to have a hard time falling asleep or would over think about work in my off hours. I love this section because it has transformed my life outside of work. It includes the following topics:

- **Flow State:** Achieving alignment between interest and challenge, where time melts away during peak performance.

- **Counterbalancing:** Pick up and put down work strategically, with high-performance juggling.

- **Cue, Craving, Response, Reward cycle (CCRR):** If our *time habits* were bricks, CCRR is the mortar in between them, the architecture of our motivation.

- **Big Gestures:** Do something grand to support a goal to help you stick with it.

- **It's okay to say no!** ... and you should probably be saying it more often.

- **The Simulator:** How our prehistoric brains keep us unnecessarily busy.

The easier we can make productivity, the better. The concepts introduced here will be helpful on their own; however, if any of these topics interest you, I encourage you to read the book cited in the section to gain a deeper understanding.

Flow State

Here you are captivated by the experience and time melts away. It's when the day ends, and you can't believe how much you got done and how fast it flew by. What a wonderful workday!

In the book *Flow: the Psychology of the Optimal Experience*, author Mihaly Csikszentmihalyi suggests that the flow state is reached when we work on tasks whose difficulty is evenly matched with our skills. Not too easy (boring), not too hard (frustrating), but appropriately challenging to be interesting.

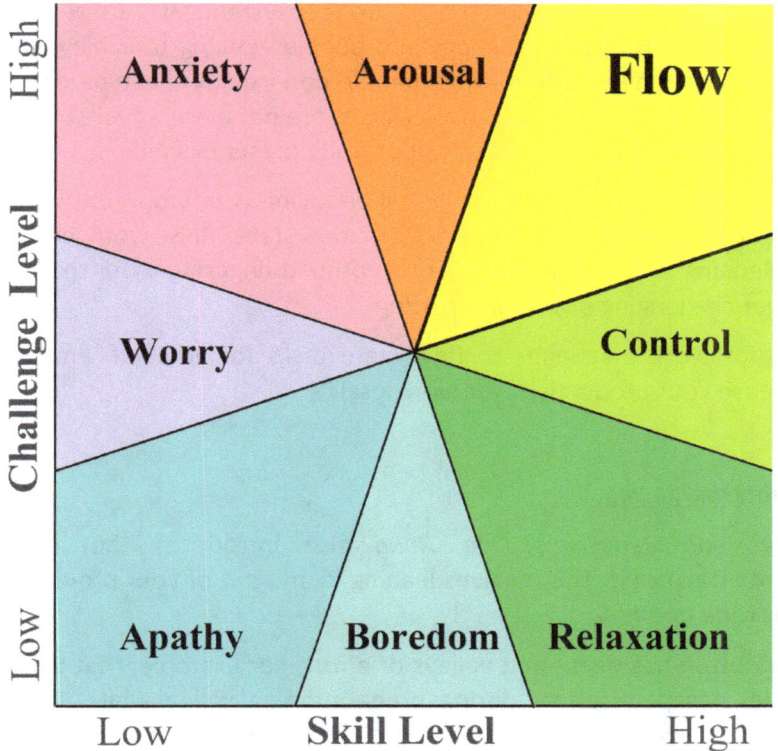

The challenge versus skill level quadrants
https://zapier.com/blog/how-to-find-flow/

This results in a blend of peak performance and general happiness. Time and the rest of the world fade away in the flow state. We produce at our maximum output because we're highly focused and the work appropriately utilizes our experience.

Consider what skills you enjoy exercising and what interests you most. The more of this type of work you can get, the more you'll outproduce an average person.

It's not always easy to define this type of work, and once you do, it can be tough to find it. Your work responsibilities won't always line up. However, attempting to identify your "flow state" work is a great start to spot the opportunities.

For example, I love designing new business systems. It's interesting to me. It's a mixture of technology and people working to achieve some goal with the new system. Most people don't enjoy this type of work, but I do, so it's a win-win. These projects are not always available, but I always raise my hand when an opportunity presents itself.

This is not to say that the result will be loving your work, but you can attempt to design your tasks toward this state. Raise your hand for challenging, interesting work. Try to offload lingering work that is no longer challenging or isn't interesting.

Aim for work that leads to flow state tasks for yourself, and you'll increase your productivity (or work less).

Counterbalancing

Keller and Papasian's *One Thing* also introduces the idea of counterbalancing. This involves leaning in and out of your projects and your **time habits**.

Work often has peaks and valleys of effort. For example, that Series A model has peak effort during preparation, a valley while it's with investors, and peaks again to address their questions and comments. I counter-balance into other high-value work during the valleys, so my **focused time** is always utilized. (When none of my jobs had peak tasks, I slowly wrote this book using excess **focused time.**)

Whether you have other high-value work to counterbalance into depends on your work strategy. The more projects you can juggle, the higher your productivity. The keyword is "can" because this must produce sufficient quality within the time constraint you'd like to devote to work.

Ninth-grade chess king captures Oklahoma's imagination
https://www.cnhinews.com/

I've maintained two remote corporate jobs for several years. As such, I always had high-value work ready and waiting on my task list. Ship the Series A model for review one day, and work on our NetSuite re-implementation on the other. This gives me plenty to do while delivering quality and usually fitting within my ideal nine-to-five workday.

Conversely, I had three roles for a while (paid great), but the overlapping peaks regularly broke my daily work time limit and made vacationing almost impossible. Consider how many projects you can effectively pick up. Too few and you're underproducing, while too many will have you overproducing. Strive for the amount that will make you most productive and happy.

In addition to daily work time limits, consider counterbalancing out of productivity entirely. That means have some time where you are not productive at all. (Gasp! How can I suggest such a thing?) This concept may be hard for some of you to grasp, so let me explain.

Most workdays fit into three descriptions:

- High production
- High touch
- None

High production is the day we modeled throughout this book. A big chunk of targeted *focused time*. Building models, writing handbooks, designing software… all the things we do in 'big brain' mode. They also include *unfocused time*, various *productive meetings*, and the *daily close*.

Conversely, there are **high touch** days. I call these face-time days and I try to lump all my in-person meetings together on these days. If I must go into an office, I'll try to force meetings into this day. I might not get any *focused time*, but high touch days help protect the other days of the week. High touch days are almost as important as high production days. Seeing people and engaging can be an x-factor to success. Until the robots take over (entirely) 😊 face time matters.

Finally, the most essential counterbalance is **"none."** Like your workday benefits by having proper boundaries, so does your work year. On weekends, fully disconnect and counterbalance *all the way out*. Schedule long weekends, full weeks off, and ideally longer if you're able. Counterbalancing into "none" is long-duration downtime, that also leads to higher performance. Enjoy it.

Cue, Craving, Response, Reward

If **time habits** were bricks, the "Cue, Craving, Response, Reward" (CCRR) cycle is the mortar. These are the microtransactions going on in the brain behind the scenes. The cycle is the catalyst for action and determines whether you do something or not. Thankfully, you're the trainer.

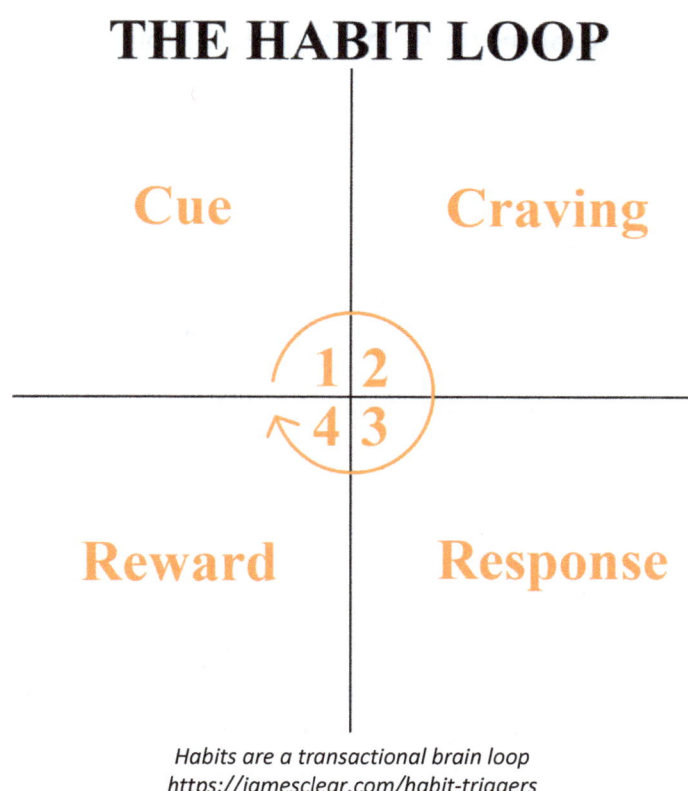

Habits are a transactional brain loop
https://jamesclear.com/habit-triggers

James Clear, Author of *Atomic Habits: An Easy & Proven Way to Build Good Habits & Break Bad Ones*, describes the process:

1. The Cue: this gets your attention and alters your focus.

2. The Craving: your brain imagines and wants the rewarding outcome.

3. The Response: you act, in hopes of receiving the reward.

4. The Reward: you get what you imagined in the craving. The habit loop is complete.

The CCRR is circular and the more often the cycle spins to completion, the more likely it will spin. Each is a transactional step in the brain, and they can be engineered, resulting in making your *time habits* and *levered task* completion even easier, if not automatic.

Cue: Make It Obvious

The cue primes you for action, and it should be obvious for *focused and unfocused time*. Adjusting the environment is a great way to start:

- Desk in standing position (or however you like)

- Lighting at preferred level (color/brightness)

- Play a warmup song

- Spray your favorite scent

- Review your *Super Day* and get to work!

There are many ways to tell your mind and body it's time for specific work. Find the best cue approach for you and incorporate it into your day.

Craving: Make it Attractive

Feeling influences action. When the cue gets you to notice it, you need to want it. When your mind finds that new state (the reward) more attractive, it will release some action dopamine.

Getting tasks done feels good. During *focused time* you'll make progress on something important. During *unfocused time* you'll complete the little stuff that must get done. Crave that sense of accomplishment, and you'll want to dive in.

You can hijack and stack cravings. In addition to desiring personal accomplishment, you can reward yourself with an extra motivator at the end of the **time habit**. Something that you personally crave the end state:

- A small treat

- An out-of-office stroll

- A spin around social media

- Talking points with your accountability partner

Ideally, your tasks are engaging, but if not, they are on your list for a reason. So getting them done and crossing them off is a great motivating craving.

Response: Make It Easy

Make it easy to achieve what you're craving. **Focused time** produces extraordinary results. Make it easy by muting interruptions, locking your phone, and committing to the tasks. Recall the various methods to make you comfortable during this time and deploy a few for yourself.

Start with manageable durations of **focused time**. My 3-hour focused chunk is awesome, but I didn't get there overnight. I started with 30 minutes at a time and grew it over the years, while training myself and slowly nudging my schedule.

Action influences feeling. Blocking your schedule and doing the tasks you outlined feels good. The more times you act, the more likely you'll do so again!

Remember, it takes around 60 days to form a new habit. Make it easy, and keep responding to the craving!

Reward: Make it Satisfying

That attractive craving must be rewarded to complete the habit-forming loop. The brain won't release action causing dopamine next time, if it doesn't expect the reward.

Habits are dopamine-driven feedback loops. Each CCRR transaction must be completed, with the last step being the reward.

If you can see the reward as being incremental movement on **big goals**, lovely. Then the reward is *doing*. The reward can be as simple as scratching items off the list. The reward can be patting yourself on the back whenever you finish big brain work.

If you need more, layer an extra motivator at the end to help incentivize your action. The point is to give your mind something it wants, after you complete the work you set out to do.

The more often you complete the loop, the better the results, and the stronger the cycle will repeat. Consider your "Cue, Craving, Response, Reward" around your **time habits** and even consider them at the goals/tasks level. Some tasks might need bigger motivators than others.

The better your habits, the better you can effortlessly control your time. As a result, you get greater productivity, allowing you to produce more and/or work less.

Big Gestures

Committing to **big goals** can be helped with big gestures, which align with your goal and represent an additional layer of commitment.

Examples of big gestures include:

- Ordering new office equipment to be comfortable during **focused time**.

- Buying a fancy calendar to put everything in one place.

- Booking a hotel room to work on a significant project.

- Sharing *Intrinsic Work* with others!

One person desired to put all their commitments on one analog calendar. They purchased a pricey leather-bound planner, which created an additional layer of commitment. Even more, they showed it off to a few people at work. It hardly mattered to those co-workers, but it created yet another layer of commitment.

On the digital side, a big gesture could be subscribing to a tie-together app to manage everything or subscribing to a booking link to make reaching out and scheduling easier. It could also be asking your significant other to send every time commitment to your calendar. When you declare that your digital calendar is your one-stop for time, it will be.

Andy Tryba made a grand gesture related to his 30-minute marble method for *focused time*. To measure the passage of time, you could use ten pennies and two plates, but Tyrba bought a monogrammed sub-divided wooden tray and polished steel bearings. This desk ornament not only looks fantastic, but serves as a grand gesture and a regular reminder of his commitment to *focused time*.

Completing any portion of this book is a grand gesture to yourself. You are serious about higher productivity and/or working less. Further, sharing the grand gesture with others cements additional commitment. (Yes, please share my book with others haha.)

When considering your goals, think about any complimentary big gestures that will help you cement your success. Doing something out of the ordinary to perpetuate commitment will increase productivity, allowing you to produce more and/or work less.

It's okay to say no!

In the *One Thing*, they say one YES should be defended by a thousand NOs. You should probably be saying NO a lot more often.

Desk sign that serves as a great reminder!

We're not always at liberty to say YES or NO to everything that comes our way. But you're probably not capitalizing on 100% of the NOs you should deploy.

NO helps to counterbalance by filtering out new juggling items. The more you try to do, the greater the risk of accomplishing less! Let your ambitious goals drive what you say YES to.

NO is helpful for everyone. Saying YES to less-than-ideal work means your productivity goes down. You're not producing maximum value, which should also be your workplace's concern. The better aligned your work with your skills, the more value they get, usually for the same paycheck.

NO helps you set better boundaries. Sometimes, people think it is easier to ask someone a question than find out the information on their own. This often occurs when one person has ownership, but the other has access ("Send me the bank statement," for example). While you may have it, this still requires you to switch modes to find it and hopefully reengage what you were doing. NO encourages people to help themselves.

"NO, I cannot attend a meeting at that time."

"NO, I cannot help with that project."

If you are not accustomed to saying NO, don't worry, you'll get better at it. Especially as your schedule becomes yours and your overall workload becomes more manageable. You'll understand how much value you give up by saying YES too often.

The Simulator

Do you ever replay or think about work situations after hours? Do you enjoy playing these movies in your mind? I don't.

They are problematic for a variety of reasons:

- Bust up recharging time

- Rarely generate groundbreaking ideas

- Distract your homelife

- Leave you paying half attention

- Keep you up at night

None of these things sound good, right? Yet you probably find yourself in this situation time and time again.

The last component in this section relates to our consciousness. Our minds. What are we thinking at any given moment? Why are we thinking about it? Do we want to be thinking about it?

I wondered if I should introduce this topic here or wait for ***Intrinsic Life***. Since work can be so pervasive, learning a bit about consciousness will be helpful. According to *Buddha's Brain: the Practical Neuroscience of Happiness, Love & Wisdom*, written by Rich Hanson, Ph.D., and Richard Mendius, M.D., we inherited a mind simulator from our ancestors.

Thousands of years ago, in a simpler world, this simulator was great for rehearsing real-life threats. Picturing a rattlesnake in the bushes helped encode the danger and response into memory. There was good chance this threat could materialize, so it gave those with strong simulators higher survival rates.

Today, our lovely simulator is bombarded with all sorts of perceived threats and opportunities, which it gloms onto and exaggerates. The great news is that the simulator can be controlled.

Anything that does not belong where it is, the way it is, is an "open loop" pulling on your attention. —https://businessentials.wordpress.com/2013/04/25/open-loops/

Solutions to calm the simulator:

- Tasks/Notes: Store in a trusted place (mind like water, as discussed)

- Journaling: get your broader thoughts into text

- Meditation: the simulator reset button

Tasks/Notes were already discussed in length earlier, so flip back to that section if you need a refresher. Sometimes you need to read things twice or even three times before the concepts set in your brain, and that's okay! The important part is absorbing the information and using it to your advantage.

Journaling can be approached in various fashions, including simple note-taking. Research techniques for yourself. It is nice if they have some structure, but the primary purpose of journaling is to get the thoughts out of your mind. Their subsequent usefulness doesn't necessarily matter. Work-related journaling could relate to some frustration or even writing about an ongoing project. Whatever keeps grabbing your mind's attention will benefit by being written out.

Meditation: The best way to control the simulator is meditation. Even the most basic meditation exercises can help quiet the mind. This will help you focus on what you want to be or help you get to sleep. *Buddha's Brain* introduces a few methods, one even as simple as focusing on your normal breathing, which is an exercise that provides big benefits in just minutes.

Meditation exercises are not difficult to learn but take time to master. Like most things, practice makes perfect. Today, if I wake up in the middle of the night thinking about something, I can quickly shrink my thoughts and go back to sleep. It feels like a superpower in comparison my old restless nights.

Truly detaching from work after hours is amazing and makes me more present. Everything is organized, and I sleep better than ever.

- Explore your Flow State work – define what interests you.

- Counterbalance – plan how much you can take on. Plan time off.

- CCRR: Plan yours for **focused time** and **unfocused time**. Create a strong habit loop.

- Big Gestures: Define a few that could help your **big goals**. Act on at least one of them.

- It's OK to say no! Remember that. Print our yes/NO sign.

- The Simulator: Find a journaling and/or a meditation method that works for you.

Case Studies

Intrinsic Work in Practice

BELOW ARE CASE STUDIES of the Intrinsic system in use based upon real-life people and real-life examples, using Intrinsic Work.

- **Mike** is a Construction Supervisor who wants to be a Partner at a family-owned construction company he has worked at for many years. Mike is new to Intrinsic Work. He's enjoying the concepts, but has had a difficult time implementing it. Nonetheless he has high hopes for using it to break free from what seems like a plateau, professionally.

- **Alan** is an Office Manager who aspires to be in leadership. He has used Intrinsic Work for several years and attributes a good amount of his success to using the system. He is ready to revisit Instrinsic Work, however, and update his planning because so many new responsibilities have been added to his role in the previous two years. He hopes to become the Chief Operating Officer of his company.

- **Craig** is a freelance writer who wants to make a living as a full-time author. He has used Intrinsic Work for just a few months, but is already seeing dramatic improvements in both his personal and professional life. His goal is to shift to being a full-time author and quit freelancing.

- **Jennifer** is an Accounting Manager who aspires to be a CFO. She has used Intrinsic Work for a year and describes her dramatic improvements. She hopes for more personal time even as she aspires for the higher role.

All of these people struggled in one way or another getting to that next stage within the timeframe they'd hoped for. We consider their backstory, their approach to *time habits*, their *big goals*, their *levered tasks* and how they *drive momentum* day-to-day and over the long haul, where real results are made.

These examples are meant to demonstrate how Intrinsic Work runs in practice, and how your life can benefit from Intrinsic Work as well. If none of these careers speak to you, our database includes many more examples at MyIntrinsicWork.com.

Mike: Construction Supervisor

Introduction

MIKE IS DEDICATED to Campbell Builders, the large family-owned construction company he works for. "In fact I started as a laborer right under Jerry Cambell fourteen years ago," he says, "and rose to Construction Supervisor within three years. He looks up from his computer, pauses for a moment, and tells me, "General Partner is what I'm gunning for now." He smiles and winks, making me think, he's not the only one in the office aware of his ambitions.

We're sitting in a construction trailer, but Mike does have an office (he swears) in their corporate headquarters in Riverview, southeast of Tampa Bay, Florida. "Big project here," he says. "Residential community and all the hardscaping has just gone in." Mike's typical day is filled with answering emails, customer meetings (both scheduled and impromptu), vendor meetings, training his team, and overseeing the people on the jobs he personally supervises. He is new to Intrinsic Work.

"So far I love it," he says, about Intrinsic Work that is. In a more serious tone he continues, giving up on his computer and swiveling his chair to address me directly. "I feel like I've learned all I can in this position, I'm ready to up my game." I get the impression Mike is an athlete just as he says "game." Although we're in a temporary or perhaps satellite office, there are pictures of Mike with a good looking family on the desk next to a (recent) trophy for what looks like softball.

"But here's the thing," he says, leaning in to me, quieter, flat-out serious, "other people seem to keep advancing while I sit here. I mean, my hopes are known, and it may just be promotions are on hold until this project is further along, but I'd like to be more confident, maybe even have thought through alternatives, should things not go the way I've been picturing." Mike's career seems to have plateaued. He gets great performance reviews and good raises, but he would love to be a legit Partner someday.

"Jerry—" at the utterance of the name Mike stops and looks at me— "*Mr. Campbell* probably would have me by his side by now, but his oldest took over just a few years ago. Good guy, but not sure where that leaves me. Maybe this system of yours can give me a leg up."

He closes his laptop and leads me from the office.

Time Habits

Mike is a manic planner. He likes his lists, and he likes checking things off his list even more. He notices me watching him consider his current to-do list. "I keep track of stats for the team here at work and the softball team, too." Another wink and a smile. He has a clear plan for each day, but he tells me, "Those plans normally get derailed the moment I get here, to the job site. In fact the drive each day is rough, out here to Pelican Harbor—that's the community we're building here. Riverview is only 30 minutes away, but that's more than an hour of driving per day. So far it's been kind of wasted time." Mike looked at me as if to say, *I know I know, Intrinsic Work!*

- At least once a week at the Peilcan Harbor site there is an inspector to entertain.
- Almost every day there are couriers to meet with to give and send architectural plans and permit applications, even though the applications are mostly handled by a third-party service.
- When Mike starts a typical day, he goes through his email. Mike is big on communication and answers everything each morning, even if it's just to say, "I'll check on this." Frequently these emails snowball into a subcontractor needing help, direction, permission, or money on a project. Mike answers these requests himself, rather than getting someone else access and training them, and then having to make sure it's done.
- As the corporate expert on procurement, he also often has people walking up to his desk, some standing in line to speak with him. Many days he does not get to his task list until after lunch, or at all if there are late meetings in the day.

And that's all at the Riverview HQ!

After learning the Intrinsic Work approach, Mike tracked an actual previous work day and it looked like this:

- Fifteen (15) minutes focused on tasks planned the day before.

- Ten (10) minutes discussing football with coworkers.

- Five (5) minutes transition time.

- Ten (10) minutes checking emails.

- Ten (10) minutes looking at news feeds that showed up in email.

- Ten (10) back on the tasks from the list.

- Followed by an hour of unplanned firefighting related to an unhappy vendor.

- Then a 10-minute walk to a meeting room…

- … followed by a 1-hour meeting.

- Then 10 extra minutes talking about sports with a meeting attendee...

- The walk back to his desk takes 30 minutes after a few more conversations on the way.

- ... followed by a 10-minute conversation about last week's parts outage.

- Then he slipped into the bathroom and took a 5-minute breather before using the facilities and heading back to his desk (a total of 15 minutes).

- He then checked social media for 10 minutes...

- ... followed by 30 minutes of focused work back on his task list...

- ... before his phone pinged and he answered people's comments about his social media post...

- ... before getting back to focused work for 20 minutes...

- ... and then going to his next meeting.

And today we can add the commute to and from Pelican Harbor to the beginning and end of it all. Can you feel the *start-stop-start-stop* in this process?

Once introduced to Intrinsic Work, Mike realized, if he wanted to get the work done, he had to train others and he'd have to train himself. He told the people at HQ and on site he'd love to talk about the big game... at lunch, cutting out his habit of "game talk" at several different points and places in the day.

Then he considered his social media usage. Stopping to make a post cost him momentum, plus the time to make the post, and then transition time to start again. Not to mention the extra time to answer people's comments.

Mike vowed to himself he'd only post during lunch—if even necessary—and not check comments until after work. He also turned off notifications to avoid the temptation of not reading every comment as they posted. He also unsubscribed from news feeds in his email. He could check news at lunch or at home.

That left *focused time*, followed by a meeting, followed by *focused time*, plus another meeting. To alleviate this start-stop routine, Mike blocked out the first hour of the day for emails and whatever questions were brewing from people, and the second hour for daily tasks on his list that he planned the day before. That gave him two solid hours of work at the beginning of the day while he was fresh, before setting off with a clear mind to Pelican Harbor.

His initial experience (remember, he's new!) has been positive and encouraging. "My head seems more clear already," he says. "What's next?"

Big Goals

While fairly new to Intrinsic Work, Mike has been at his current role and company a relatively long time. We discussed his current *big goals* as well as his current situation.

"I get it," he says, "full Partner might not be in the stars. I guess I didn't factor in the family element when I used to look forward. It's a bit of a shame but I guess I understand, if I had a son and a successful company... But that's just the way it is. So, when I really looked at things realistically, yes, I love this company, I love what I do, and I'm good at it. Heck, I've been around as long as anyone, but it may be time to lean into my success at something new."

We were walking the site now, a daily ritual for Mike when he's here, making his presence and availability known to all on site.

"There he is!" Mike shouts with a smile, toward a man with a hardhat who is looking up at several framers working on the roof. The man turns and with a smile of recognition waves Mike off, then goes back to overseeing the work.

Component Goals

"Making partner at CB is how I'd define success at my current company, but I think I need an alternate goal, Andrew. What if this is as far as I go here? I'd want my own show, so starting my own business is my other component goal.

Annual Goals

The first goal requires staying the course, getting even more efficient with the help of Intrinsic Work, keeping his role met and expectations exceeded where possible, while also looking *up* at the possibility of becoming a Partner with a stake in the company. That likely means more familiarity with the ins and outs of the company, which while private, has issued stock and has several investors, affiliate companies, "corporate stuff," as Mike says.

"For the second goal, I'll need my general contractor's license. In fact I wouldn't be shocked if that's a roadblock for me right now here and they're just not telling me because if I did go to the trouble and *not* get promoted I'd probably resent the effort, and if I did get licensed I could easily leave. It's these kinds of calculations I never fully pondered until I had some written goals in place."

As far as getting his license, Mike not only needs to take a prep course and study materials for a state exam, he needs a licensed sponsor. "Oh, Jerry will do that, no problem," he says. "And, I framed it through me wanting to be ready to move up, I didn't mention anything about maybe starting my own thing."

Another wink and a smile, as he hands me a printout on his clipboard. "For starting my own thing, my primary annual goal is related to that GC license. Once it's started and certainly as it nears completion, that goal will get more detailed about actually starting a business."

Itemized

Big Goal
Ownership Interest in a Residential Building Company

Component Goals

1. **Partner at Campbell Builders.**
2. **Start my own company.**

Annual Goals ~ Partner at Campbell Builders

A. **Maintain excellence in current job** (meet or beat deadlines and budgets).
B. **Stay in excellent communication** with upper management (Campbell Family), affiliates, and subcontractors.
C. **Learn the Corporate Stuff**—stock value? Strategic planning, etc.
D. **Make this newfound know-how *and my licensing apparent*** in conversations with Jerry Jr. (Heck, he'll have to hire or fire me either way!)

Annual Goals ~ Licensed General Contractor

A. **Learn the requirements for licensure** in Florida and obtain the needed study materials.
B. **Start prep course**.
C. **Schedule state exam**.
D. ***PASS state exam!***

Levered Tasks Example for One Annual Goal

The how, when, and where are the **levered tasks**. For Mike, some of the tasks he uncovered actually seemed "silly" or questionable at first, but when he examined the purpose of positioning himself for Partnership (at Campbell, elsewhere or his own thing) he realized he needed to associate more with the executives in his company, not to "kiss up" but to network and learn from them.

This new perspective traveled down to his **levered tasks** ideas, as you will see in the chart that follows. Mike was surprised, in his case, to see how important certain socialization actually was, over and above his actual performance at work. And for Mike, as for most people, the act of defining **levered tasks** gels it all together.

Here's how it looks for Mike if we look at his **component goal** of becoming a Partner at Campbell Builders and is **annual goal** is to Learn the Corporate Stuff:

Levered Tasks	Time Habits			
	Focused Time	**Unfocused Time**	**Meetings**	**Downtime**
Annual Goal: Learn the Focus & Actions of a Partner	Access and study previous Board meetings.	Watch videos (during lunch, breaks, etc.) of successful executives and their stories.	Special attention paid to meetings with upper-level people within the organization, including Jerry Jr. Board members, etc. Meet when possible.	Schedule lunch once per quarter with current Partners.
	Understand current long-term vision for Campbell. Study contemporary proven business practices, notably those used by private equity.		Travel to annual and periodic company meetups as much as possible, especially those of an executive nature.	

Mike's Driving Momentum

If you'll recall from Part 4: Drive Momentum …

> **_"Driving momentum_** involves daily planning,
> accountability methods, and helpful tools that propel
> day-to-day production."

Daily Planning

"There's no way around my daily trips from Riverview to Peilcan Harbor," starts Mike, "but when I saw what you wrote about **time habits** I kind of gave myself a break, maybe even in a weird way. I mean, I used to have a dash of worry, like that ride simply took away from my productivity, but realizing **unfocused time** can be an asset has me at ease with it now. _It's unfocused time! Perfect!_ And now that I've thought through it I see how I'm being productive during that daily ride. And if I call my wife it's valid downtime."

Yep, a wink and a smile.

"And when it comes to daily planning it's all now organized versus just kind of smashed together. So I arrive in Riverview each day … well you'll see what I'm talking about with my **_SUPER DAY._**"

Mike flipped his clipboard around—it was the aluminum storage type— and showed me what he was talking about.

Super Day

Reminder: This exercise can be done analog or digital, whichever you prefer. I like planning my **Super Day** using the Intrinsic Work application available on MyIntrinsicWork.com. I print mine to a physical copy to give myself an itinerary to look at and scribble notes on. Conversely, some people use the template in PDF or just put everything on their digital calendar. Mike's sample **Super Day** follows after this example.

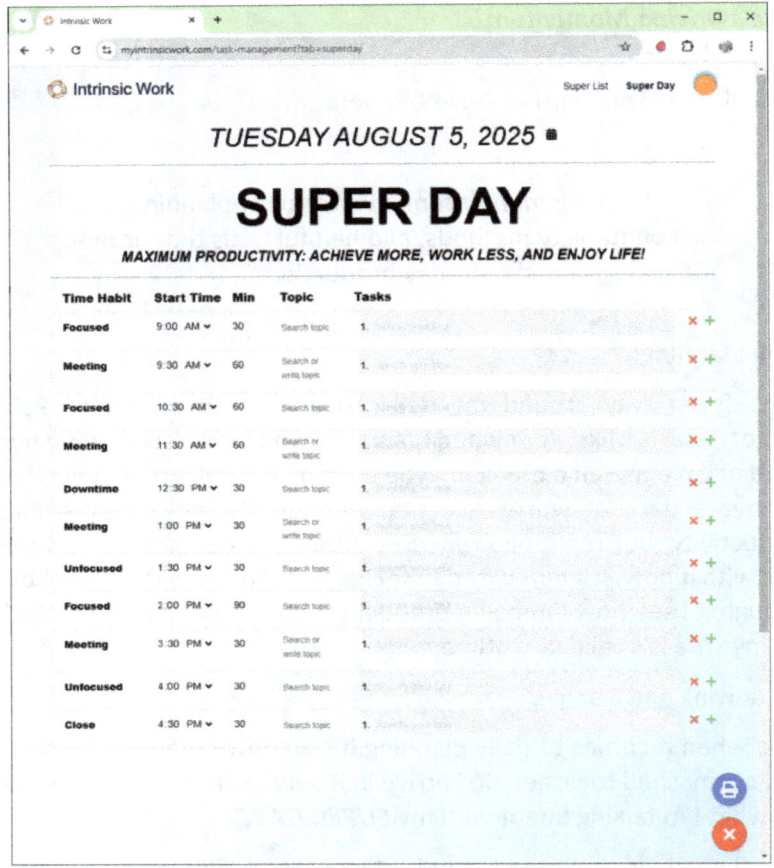

App available by visiting www.MyIntrinsicWork.com

Daily Close

"At the end of the day the first thing I do is check emails, texts, and my inbox at Pelican Harbor again, just to make sure I have not missed anything urgent, especially if it helps me avoid having to go back to Riverview before morning. I used to do that and it was killing me. And with a look at what tomorrow might bring I find the ride home is actually enjoyable, usually, and I have been sleeping better, while also—here's the kicker—making actual progress using this system each day toward my big goal of advancing, at Campbell or anywhere."

Mike looks me in the eye, maybe the most serious I've seen him, and says, "You know what? For maybe the first time I feel like I'm not just coping but working on *me,* and that makes me feel like I'm actually going to do this, I'm going to have a career I'm happy with. It's kind of a big deal. So, thanks, Andy—sorry, can I call you Andy?"

I tell him in this case that's fine, and I give Mike a smile and a wink.

Accountability

"Well, my wife is truly my better half. She's more intent on my progress than I think I am, and that's not any kind of gold-digging, she just knows what it means to me. To have someone in your corner like that is fundamental to your success, if you can swing it. We discuss work all the time, but it's much happier talk lately, ha!"

Mike also explains that he's been open with his boss, Jerry Jr., about his hopes with Campbell, and that Jerry gets it, even if the advance is not necessarily imminent. "It's helped me really want to put my money where my mouth is, and so far so good," he says.

Helpful Tools

"What helps, and this might or might not sound goofy, is first and foremost my stupid clipboard. Man, I lost this thing once... and I thought I wasn't going to make it! But it's all in here and it's all with me all the time. If it doesn't fit in here it's not worth having. I've also added a music subscription to my car audio and that's been so much more than entertainment—You'd be surprised what these 'little things' can do for yourself once you consider what you can do in **unfocused time**.

"The other thing that comes to mind? You really want to know? I really believe people see me as a friendly guy, but they also see how busy I am. My wife got me a little metal sign with a bulldog on it that says *Who Goes There? Can this be sent by email?* It's reduced the random traffic in my mornings *by half*."

Mike, how's it going?

Mike found that dedicating himself to those carved-out **focused work** periods and corralling his random walk-ins increased his productivity by almost fifty percent! Where he was barely getting one task done a day before, between all the random chats and commuting, now he was getting two or three tasks done in the morning alone!

In Mike's case, he's carved out meeting time at Peilcan Harbor to connect with direct reports and peers, while he created a 30-minute window to meet the big wigs back at HQ every day, and it's been working beautifully, he says.

His days are not always perfect. He does still get interrupted sometimes, in the mornings especially, but as long as he sticks to this schedule most days, he finds he's able to get more work done in one or two days than he used to get done in a week, and he still has time in the afternoons for coworkers to call on his expertise.

On Fridays, if all is on-time and on- or under-budget at the site, Mike has petitioned to be able to come back to HQ and study for his contractor's license the rest of the day without interruption. And he often gets to do it. In fact, he found of all the places he seems to spend his time, Fridays in Riverview are the quietest, and this has added a lot of fuel to his studies. He feels great knowing where he's heading.

Alan: Office Manager

Introduction

ALAN IS AN office manager at a large automotive industry parts manufacturing company outside of Detroit, Michigan. He has been in this role for three years, and he likes it, but he is very busy. "I've been using the system, Intrinsic Work, for the whole time I've been here," he says. He leads me along a metal walkway, overlooking the manufacturing floor. Amidst the beeps and constant sirens and clanks, he half shouts what he's saying as we walk. From time-to-time he turns to me, as if making sure I'm getting what he says. "I credit Intrinsic Work with my pretty rapid progress here," he says. He has received excellent reviews and raises along the way, but he wants to achieve a bigger role someday. His dream is to be a Chief Operating Officer, the COO, helping to also make everything work properly, but at a much higher level. "So,

I've revisited my Intrinsic Work planning, stepping up my game," he says.

The office manager role requires him to be in contact with a core group of people, along with random interactions with almost anyone. The result tends to be a lot of pop-up items, daily to-dos, a few meetings, and the usual emails, texts, and other communications from people with office needs. "I don't see this as a big obstacle. I guess I have confidence because I can already envision how, if I revisit my Intrinsic Work plans, I can put things back in place that have maybe slipped a bit with the evolution of my duties here." He turns to me, "Make that the *addition of duties* I have here," and he cracks a smile.

Lately Alan tends to have somewhat scattered days. He has been given the technical project of planning an upcoming investor hosting event, which requires many meetings, vendor outreach calls, and all sorts of additional time demands. His typical day, these days, is "high-touch, low productivity" after several years of growth, he's departed from his original Intrinsic Work plan.

But despite the circus it seems to be at times, Alan always seems to get it done. He mostly works long hours in the office and is often the first to arrive and the last to leave. "I'm glad you're here," he says with a fist-bump to my shoulder as he guides me into his office. "You're making me take the planning more seriously, and I need that now."

Time Habits

If most office workers have scattered days, Alan's looks twice as bad. While he also describes his day using the "stock" Intrinsic framework, he identified many more slices and occurrences, most of which was not *focused time*. Similarly to what we will see with our Accounting Manager, Jennifer, Alan was responding to everything and thus not performing meaningful time habits. He had slipped, let daily "distraction creep" sort of dissolve the better time habits he had two years ago.

Calling out *time habits* allowed Alan to be cognizant of them, and to consider how he might fit them into his day. For *focused time*, he decided to create a do-not-disturb window on his email and phone.

After some trial and error, he found **focused time** is best attempted at the end of the day.

"I meet the busy day head-on, answer "urgent" requests, attend meetings, and take a real lunch. Usually, there is more chaos after lunch, and then I rope off 2-3 hours for a **focused time** at the end of the day."

Upon taking the Office Manager position two years ago, Alan let people know about his scheduling routine, thanks to adopting Intrinsic Work at that time, and for the most part, people adjusted their expectations. "Now," he says, "I need to train the people around me, because people, especially new people, stop by unannounced, call when it's not important, and schedule meetings at whatever time they please. But it's getting better. Hey, maybe that's the next level in this process."

He started nudging recurring meetings and events into the morning and grouped them where possible. He mostly now achieves his **focused time** goal each day.

At least one day a week he walks into a line shut down. An assembly line stopping means the company won't be profitable that day, and workers will be standing around, getting paid without producing. Alan has good people, but upper management requires him to get involved in a shutdown situation, and that involvement doesn't end until the line is back up and running. Point being, real life still gets in the way from time to time and that's okay.

Overall, Alan feels he's benefitted greatly, but it's time to readjust. "Look, I should know, I've been using the system for two years at least. So I'll definitely take a fresh look at **focused time, unfocused time, meetings**, and God willing, **downtime**.

Big Goals

While Alan is currently in the Office Manager role at the plant, he aspires for management, specifically the Chief Operating Officer role. He enjoys his current company, and they have promoted people all the way to the top from within before. He's willing to stay where he is for an opening, but if not, he's prepared to seek a role at another manufacturing company, or even in a whole new field should the opportunity present itself. He's ambitious, and wants an opportunity for long-term growth.

When considering what might be done in the upcoming year, *if he had the time*, Alan would like to get more involved with the operations side of the business. As an office manager, he is exposed to a bit of everything, but he would like some real targeted experience.

Alan's boss agreed that these extracurricular goals would be great to pursue and was excited to figure out how to get him this experience. Ultimately, they agreed to make them part of Alan's official goals, which would help the large organization respond appropriately.

Component Goals

As it related to success at his current company, Alan developed the following **component goals** he'd like to pursue:

Itemized

Big Goal
Chief Operating Officer at Current Company or Other

Component Goals
1. **Success at current gig** furthered by continuation of what has been working, including updating my Intrinsic Work profile/framework for moving forward efficiently, particularly with new employees unaware of how I manage encounters.
2. **Success at something new** Consolidate Aptitude, Skills, Experience, and Goals for Presentation (resume + confidential outreach) to further a crisp career path either with current conglomerate or a new company.

Annual Goals ~ Success at Current Gig

A. **Update Intrinsic Work** framework, refresh *time habits* policies with people, and use the ***Super Day*** every day.
B. **Safety policy**: Work with the operations manager and others as needed to enhance our safety policy.
C. **Annual budget**: Work with the operations manager and the finance team on the upcoming annual budget. Understand how our piece of spend fits within the overall picture and how best to manage it.

Annual Goals ~ Consolidate Credentials

A. Update resume.
B. Engage recruiter services for new opportunities, at first confidentially.

Levered Tasks Example for One Annual Goal

Alan spoke to his management team about the goals outlined related to his current job, along with the Head of Manufacturing and the Head of Accounting who all welcomed the help. Below is Alan's Goal/Time/Task mapping for his ***annual goal*** of *Safety Policy* detailing tasks that can be done within the given ***time habits***:

Levered Tasks		Time Habits			
		Focused Time	Unfocused Time	Meetings	Downtime
Annual Goal: Develop Safety Policy	Content	1. Review current policy note potential changes. 2. Research best practices. 3. Craft new policy.	1. Read articles discovered during research. 2. Talk to people in the field to understand the real safety world concerns.	Meet with the Head of Manufac-turing to discuss progress.	Listen to the "WorkSAFE" podcast.
	Approval	4. Submit proposal to seniors. 5. Amend as needed.	3. Seek out similar programs in other companies for info.	Meet with executives re for approvals.	Have lunch with the boss to discuss progress.
	Imple-mentation	6. Craft & distribute email. 7. Ask & consider feedback.	4. Read "The Five Dysfunc-tions of a Team" to learn more about leadership.	Attend weekly safety meetings.	Discuss informally with staff once active.

As you can see, Alan's tasks are designed to guide and focus his efforts. They don't necessarily have every little detail and motion, but they are the broad pieces to keep his daily efforts on track.

Alan's Driving Momentum

Daily Planning

Alan has been working on the Intrinsic system for just under three years. Long-duration **focused time** was a big struggle for all the usual reasons. First, he had to train himself.

"Breaking bad habits was the hard part for me. Even while I was doing something (like doom-scrolling the internet) I knew it was a waste of time. But I still couldn't stop myself. Eventually, I found that while scrolling was fun, I didn't really miss it once it was out of my life. I found it was even more relaxing to do on the weekend, or while I was waiting for my kid's soccer game to start."

Alan also had to train those around him.

"Boy, did I get push back at first. Everyone wanted that little bit of free time I had. What I ended up doing was scheduling a 'meeting' for my focused time. For the most part, that gave me the time I needed to get actual work done. Let's face it; things aren't perfect," Alan admits.

Super Day

"Sure, I've used the Super Day for a few years now, and I love it. My brother-in-law first used the word *switching* with me, and the Super Day all but eliminates it."

SUPER DAY

MAXIMUM PRODUCTIVITY: ACHIEVE MORE, WORK LESS, AND ENJOY LIFE!

Time Habit	Start Time	Minutes	Goals & Tasks (circled when done)
Unfocused	7:00 a.m.	60:00	• Leave home for office. • (downtime) Listen to audiobooks of personal choice.
Meeting	8:00 a.m.	30:00	• Arrive at plant. • Daily exec/management meeting.
Unfocused	8:30 a.m.	3 hours	• *Conditional: Reach out to check on any possible line shutdowns and as possible delegate restoration accordingly.* • Check, answer all emails, inbox comms, voicemails, notes from assistant/secretary • Daily plant "walkabout" for performance, quality control, any employee or line issues observed (one of largest duties).
Meeting	11:30 a.m.	30:00	• "Open door time," employees on notice of this by standing memo.
Lunch	12:00 p.m.	60:00	• *Lunch as possible/needed with employees/area supervisors, execs, or if needed alongside voice or video conference with inspectors, etc.*
Focused	1:00 p.m.	3 hours	• Any wrap-ups as needed from day so far. • (current major project) Investor Event prep. • Focus on methods of maintaining and/or improving line function and efficiency. • Read guidance on any new plant requirements, safety protocols, etc. as required by (new) code.
Close	4:00 p.m.	30:00	• Comb emails, update task list and plan tomorrow's *Super Day*

Daily Close

Alan's daily framework seems to keep his Daily Close rather simple, as much of his management role consists of monitoring facets of the plant throughout the day. Many of his days look alike, but as he says, "Nonetheless I've found the daily close to be invaluable for clarity and detaching from work."

Accountability

"I've never had a problem with this (accountability)," Alan says. "I've always been pretty good solo, but my partner does help very much with keeping a 30,000-foot view of things and where we're going. That has a lot to do with mutual interest, I guess. He also has ambitions—he works for a large corporation and has his own big dream about moving upward. So I guess that's my biggest source of accountability."

Helpful Tools

To keep it all going, Alan deployed a number of tactics from **Part 4: Drive Momentum**. He plans and prints his *Super Day* at the end of every workday and he relies on the Super List to help him keep track of his tasks and prioritize them.

He deploys the *Super Week* as a check-off list. He prints it and keeps it at the top-right of his desk. At the end of each day he circles when the time habit is done successfully. Sometimes they aren't, and that's okay. Additionally, when preparing the *Super Week*, he blocks his calendar the following week for any time habits that are not already on the recurring list. This allows for more meeting availability leading up to the week and then less availability during the week.

As if taking a lesson from Jennifer, our accounting manager (case study upcoming), Alan tied his personal and work calendars together to make *at a glance* scheduling easier. He also requested his partner send him an invite for all family events—even if it was just a request to "pick up milk on the way home." At first his partner thought this strange, but then they realized that if it was on his calendar, Alan didn't forget.

Alan, how's it going?

Like our other case studies, coworkers still double-schedule meetings when he doesn't want them, stop by unannounced, and otherwise derail his plans. This isn't a problem though, as long as he always goes back to his plan. Ideally, you want every day to work perfectly, but the value in *Intrinsic Work* is that it still helps, even on those bad days and weeks.

Alan is finding that he is now able to take vacation days instead of simply losing them at the end of each year. He and his partner even took their first "unplugged" vacation in five years!

As for his trajectory, after gaining sales and manufacturing experience, he talked to HR and let them know he was ready for more responsibility (hint, hint ... COO). While they admitted he'd grown beyond his job title, they simply had nothing for him at the time. So he got to work defining his dream job outside of his current company, and thanks to his preparation he is ready for even for that scenario.

This involved a combination of soul-searching and looking through what kinds of positions were available. After about 12 months of research and interviewing (including rejecting a few job offers that were not a good fit), Alan found a job at a Fortune 500 manufacturing firm, taking on their brand new role of VP of Safety. It involved a three-hour move, but it put Alan an hour closer to his family, and his partner was happy to continue working remote in a new location.

It turned out to be a win-win for both of them!

Craig: Freelance Writer

Introduction

CRAIG STARTED OVER at the tender age of 40, after his real estate offices went bust along with the market bubble in Florida 15 years ago. Since then he has gratefully built a practice as a freelance writer, getting much of his business from online platforms like Upwork and Reedsy in addition to the referrals he receives. While writing for a living is a dream, and his colleagues are often jealous of how busy Craig is, it has been an often frantic lifestyle, nonetheless.

Given the above, Craig has often rationalized his business with gratitude for an unusual lifestyle full of freedoms, and coveted by "office dwellers," but Craig realized something had to change, and he discovered Intrinsic Work only several months ago. He's excited at the prospect that this could mean not only an easier-to-manage lifestyle with more free time, but actual progress toward his bigger goal of becoming a full-time author. Since starting Intrinsic Work, Craig has seen dramatic improvement in his day-to-day progress. While still remarkably busy, what has changed is he now has the time to work on non-paying activities that are investments in his larger vision, in addition to managing his "day job" of freelance writing projects.

"It actually feels like I'm going to make it, now," he says. "And the business is actually kind of welcome, because I used to feel like I was stuck on a hamster wheel of work—find new clients, work, find new clients, never stops. Mine is a practice that is hard to systemize, hard to delegate. So this is encouraging!" He says that with a new sense of optimism based on results because he can see the progress in the other fronts he has wanted to develop for so long. "While they might seem very synergistic, writing for others and building a career as an author are different enough," he laughs. "I once shifted from owning a small construction business to being a full-time real estate agent, and it was a hard-fought year, but it worked, so the extra effort is nothing new, as long as I can see real progress."

Time Habits

Craig's day used to be rife with switching, time wasters, distractions, and meetings, usually by Zoom, peppered all throughout his week, each one a mental shift in itself that interfered with his ability to focus on a given project. "It created a nasty burn in my stomach," he says. "But of course, you smile and give each person you deal with your best, even if each conference was filled with a sense of burnout."

In fact, it was burnout that worried Craig the most. "I really love what I do and in fact always wanted to do more of it; to learn more related skills, to make new colleagues and connections, to stay abreast of the industry and the opportunities, and I knew from experience that compromising or cheating that in any way could be the seeds of destruction in what I love doing. Shifting to writing has been a dream, and I was starting to worry that after all these years, although successful in almost every sense, I was doomed to move on for sheer economics or even worse, physical and mental fatigue."

Some of Craig's identified time habits before Intrinsic Work used to include:

- Doing high value work. Those precious periods where he could put headphones on to smooth jazz, force himself to get started, and flow, reminded of how much he loves to write, how much he loves the final product and presenting it to a client.
- Administering what he does—his method of keeping work notes and time logs, seeking out better, more efficient practices, learning new skills and bettering his craft.
- Making time to read, often in small chunks, and often, he admits, "sneaking a book with me into the restroom."
- In-between every task, checking emails, at times to be upset by a sense of overload, or going fully off-track and addressing them.
- A habit of touching a series of websites, some work-related, some author-related, and too many small "checks" on social media—something he knew deep down was costing more time than he cared to admit or even measure.
- Maybe worst of all, as ideas, communications, and needed tasks presented themselves, Craig, in the name of "being organized," usually wrote it down, created a list to be prioritized—all time spent "organizing" versus actually producing. An author he helped in the past taught him to "80/20" his daily tasks, and focus on the "20," but even that seemed like it would require more administration than he could bare.
- Craig knew to take frequent breaks, even short ones, as when he started this more sedentary work life he found it took a physical toll. So about every hour he would try to get up and walk, stretch, do the laundry, anything to move around, in order to get back to his laptop with a renewed sense of energy.
- All the while "down time" seemed lacking, and he was often plagued by guilt in spending more time with his wife or daughter, unless they had a short vacation planned and he could work around the clock in anticipation of the event.

Upon finding Intrinsic Work, it was a revelation to categorize all of the above into:

- Focused time
- Unfocused time
- Meetings, and
- Downtime

After doing so, Craig says, "It was actually quite easy to allocate these things. In fact just the act of doing so revealed time spent in places I didn't need to, and it really brought home how much *switching* was killing me, every day. I think of all the time wasted before Intrinsic Work that could have been better spent with my daughter, my wife, reading— and *not* by sneaking a book into the bathroom, or heck, better spent standing on the beach and doing … nothing. But now? I've seen the Promised Land and I can't go back!"

Big Goals

Craig's goal has been and still is to be a full-time author. That involves measurable things Craig is well aware of, but they are often outside of his daily necessary work of writing for others. He explains, "That includes successful advertising on Facebook and Amazon, procuring guest podcast appearances and starting and growing my own podcast channel, maintaining and growing a monthly email newsletter, and most of all, writing more books!"

I asked about his long-term, component, and annual goals, and he smiled. He sorted through the papers clamped into a clipboard, found one, and read them to me.

"Big goal: full-time author. That means a sufficient backlist of books, a sizeable email list, advertising acumen, an active podcast and making guest appearances, and always learning new skills. And, of course, something to write about."

We laughed at that one.

Component Goals

"I've broken this into two **component goals***:* First, success at my current gig. While I am self-employed, I'd still like to shift this from what I do now, to being a full time author. But while I earn a living, I might as well get the most out of it! I consider this to be anything that might overlap with my second component goals, the buildout for becoming a full-time author. If I can help someone, or at least see how they build (or fail) at building their list, for example, it will add value. I can earn a living, while chasing projects that overlap and align even more with my second component goal. For example, I've added the podcasting agency facet to what I offer other authors, and it's something I wanted to start doing for myself, anyway.

"And yes, this system has been holistic for me. On the second component goal of becoming a full time author there are three annuals goals that lineup—(1) a backlist or probably seven books in one genre, (2) an email list of 10,000 people—not a cheap one either, one that has accumulated, gathered a tribe of folks who want my next book, and (3) the infrastructure that supports it all. That means a website but much more—a way of selling books direct to readers, gathering emails, and the promotional actions proven to make *an author viable.* Maybe instead of 'infrastructure' I'd better say *platform.* So, list, books, platform." Craig nodded, sipped his venti iced mocha, leaned his elbows on the table and considered it all as he gazed out the window and said, "Yeah, that's it!" He looked back at me with a nod, "Simple, right? Yet I hesitated to *start* until it seemed I had a way, and that way was Intrinsic Work. It's the only paradigm I've found that has afforded me the ability to both work my day job, progress my dream job, and be a presence in my wife and daughter's lives."

Craig showed me another page in his clipboard...

Itemized

Big Goal
Full-time author

Component Goals

1. **Success at current gig** with more and more overlap to being an author, myself.
2. **Build an author career** by reaching 7 related titles, 10,000 email subscribers, and operational infrastructure that supports it all.

Annual Goals ~ Success at Current Gig

A. Maintain income and excellence with current client list (measured in feedback, reviews and earnings).
B. Research needed functions for career authors, learn and get results with them, and offer these as services to others in my practice, achieving almost complete overlap by the end of the year.

Annual Goals ~ Build an Author Career

A. With two books published already, **publish two more books** this year en route to having seven.
B. Create a newsletter, offer it with an incentive to readers for signing up, and **grow my email** list to equal or exceed 2,500 people.
C. Build a **functioning platform** including a website that sells books directly, incentivizes people to subscribe to emails, and shares news and events (this should actually be done first), supported by ads, appearances, and a newsletter.

Levered Tasks Example for One Annual Goal

So, *how* does he do it? Goals are great but the how, when, and where are important too. That's where our **levered tasks** come in.

"Okay, so I took my big goal, broke it into those two component goals, then set annual goals under those, but it's the specifics of the levered tasks that make it really clear. If a new task presents itself during the day, it either aligns with what you're working on or it does not. And what you don't do is as important as what you do do. I hope that makes sense! And, the world has opened up for me, ironically, by clamping down in certain ways. The way I see it, you start big and keep breaking things down until you know what you need to do every day."

As with Craig, for most people the act of defining **levered tasks** gels it all together. Here's how it looks for Craig as we follow one of his stated *annual goals,* "publish two more books." Considering this *annual goal*, what tasks could be done within the given *time habits*?

"And," Craig offers, flipping pages. He finds what he's looking for, eager to share, "here we go, **levered tasks** according to time habits. Here are the tasks I have for the publishing books goal."

Levered Tasks		Time Habits			
		Focused Time	Unfocused Time	Meetings	Downtime
Annual Goal: Publish Two More Books	**Write**	1. Find a new editor. 2. Buy & master Scrivener. 3. Improve daily word count.	Listen to podcasts relevant to topic Read articles of possible relevance.	Of highest relevance only—editor(s), subject interviews, etc.	Read! ... for relevance as well as pleasure. Attend appearances of other authors.
	Publish	4. Design book cover. 5. Format for publishing. 6. Upload to platforms.	Watch videos on improving publishing process. Seek out conversation re publishing.	Cover and book designers.	Browse bookstores and see what's new, how published, formatted.
	Promote	7. Create launch team. 8. Plan launch party. 9. Place ads in social media.	Always have business cards and copies of books on hand to give out.	Ad accounts, marketers, etc.	Watch any and all podcasts for ideas.

Craig explained all of this was just in relation to his big goal of full-time author, that Intrinsic Work, while now promoting his big goal and his progress towards it, was what first freed him up to have the luxury of even considering doing things that furthered this goal.

"Oh, yeah, wow," he says, "I'd still be sweating out the next client, the next project deadline, and have no chance at even doing these things, much less ever seeing my wife had I not shifted paradigms. I've done the same exercises for my business and then some. For example, as I acquire new author-related skills, I now offer them as a service to existing clients and others as needed. It's shifted my whole operation actually, and I no longer need *new* clients. I'm really closing in, thanks to this philosophy. And it's not rocket science. I've even found things to delegate to a virtual assistant, or automate with software, like time tracking and billing."

Driving Momentum

Daily Planning

"Paper. On my old-fashioned clipboard. Maybe I'm old, maybe I spend far too much time in front of a screen for other people, but I literally draw my Super Day on a nice, blank, white paper I keep on a clipboard with me at basically all times. Progressive, eh?"

Craig smiles, but I assure him his adoption of Intrinsic Work is progressive enough. And of course, it's his results that matter. He reaches into his backpack and pulls out the clipboard he must have been referring to, hands it to me. I see what he means—he really does draw it himself.

Gently shoving his latte aside, he leans across the table and points at the page atop the clipboard.

He explains, "See what I mean? The hard part, actually, was, once my time was organized, sticking to the plan. But I did. For one thing, *all calls and conferences* I vigilantly now limit to Tuesdays and Thursdays. It gives me the rest of the week for actual, relaxed and uninterrupted *production.* Imagine that! And, if I need to accelerate business, I just go to three days of calls instead of two to invite more intro calls, then back to the two as soon as possible."

With the past now "in the past," Craig is excited by how he manages his typical day.

"This actually makes my Super Day even simpler. I usually have so many appointments they literally fill all of Tuesday and Thursday, enough that if *all I did* was have *productive* meetings those days it's fine, I've been productive. And the other three days in my work week are generally free of interruptions and way less switching from randomly timed meetings that were destroying my days—my life!"

Craig hands over his latest Super Day "Rather than your achieve more, work less quote, I like to put my own cool quote each day on mine."

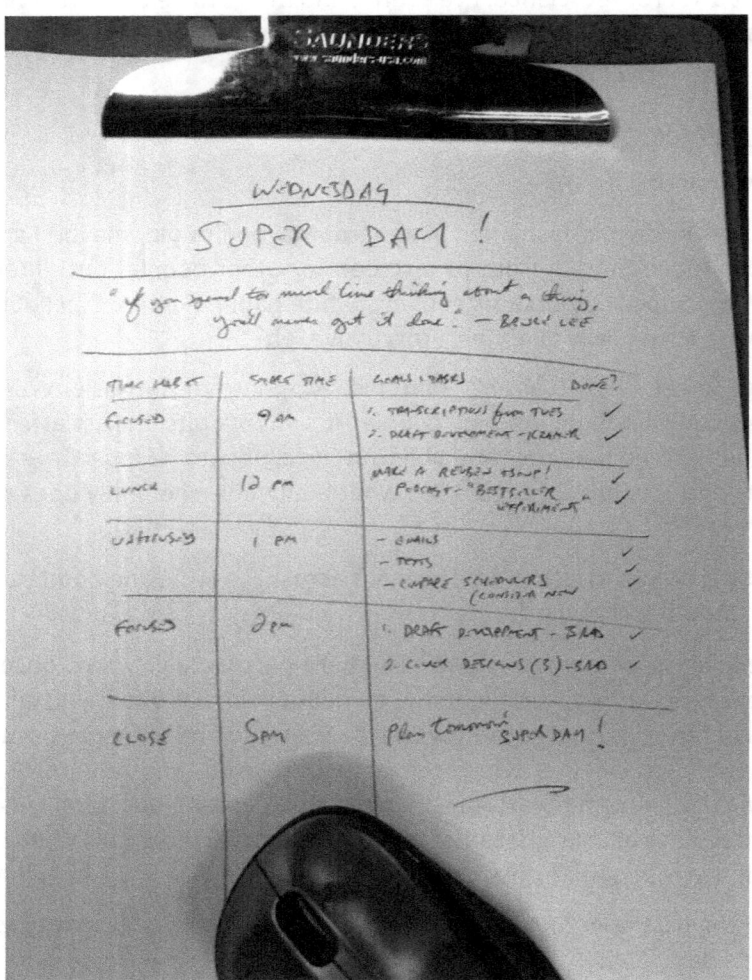

Daily Close

"At the end of each day," he says, "I'll wrap what I'm working on and spend a little time looking at tomorrow. Between my calendar, my current projects as an author, my client list, and any personal priorities, I make a quick list under each of those as headings, in that order to keep my priorities straight. It's clearly now *organized,* whereas I used to simply *cope* through life and everything always seemed like an emergency. Blecch. There's a bit of pressure, to tell you the truth, making sure I spend at least *some time* on my author path whenever possible. I used to work client projects literally all the time. That would be fine if I had no other ambitions, I mean, what I do is pretty great as it is, but I tried it that way, and made zero progress for years. Not anymore.

"And one day I made a breakthrough. I searched for some time management tips and this fellow said to *schedule, don't just list,* and it's changed my life. So after I make the list by each prioritized category, above that I make a schedule for Tuesday, for example, on Monday. And I can sleep at night.

"And then I found the Super Day. It's what I was doing on steroids."

Accountability

"I've had it pretty easy, actually," Craig says. "My wife noticed I was sleeping better. Well, one day she asked me what was up. I showed her my clipboard. I told her I was managing my gigs better, and at the end of each day doing one of these Super Day planners, and it cleared my head for the off-hours. She told me I had to keep doing them! No worries, I told her, I've been on it a month, or whatever it was, but it was becoming a favorite habit."

Helpful Tools

"And," Craig tells me, with a sense of closure, "I have my admin to a minimum, which is just where I want it, thanks to these ***trusted systems***:

- "I use iCal integrated with Calendly and it's on auto-pilot, for the most part as far as a calendar,

- "I no longer list some things. Unless it's a large task, for example, when an email comes in I *do it there and then.* This alone has helped tremendously.

- "For notes ... you guessed it!" Craig lifts the clipboard sitting between us. "Scratch notes, mini checklists. Otherwise it's all in my Super Day."

- "The one other things I really enjoy now is quick communication. What I mean is, when I check my email I *answer all of them quickly.* That might look like *Thank you, I'm on this tomorrow,* or whatever, but it's removed a chunk of anxiety I used to carry around, feeling like I'm 'good' with everyone I'm working with. It's what I like anyway, when I'm on the other end of things."

How's it Going

"It all sounds so simple now, and it is, but many never get to it. The cobbler's kids and all that. It takes time to grow a backlist, to grow a list of readers and engage a community of people who will buy your books. But I know there's a tipping point, where it makes more sense to work on these things than work for others. And I can finally see it happening, *for real.*"

When I talked to Craig I was struck by his non-chalance, by his carefreeness. We met for a coffee and I asked him about all of this, and his body language was not that of the stressed-out freelancer he describes.

"Ha!" he says, "That seems like another life."

Jennifer: Accounting Manager

Introduction

JENNIFER IS AN accounting manager at a mid-sized company in the oil and gas sector based in Longview, Texas. She has been in this role for seven years, during a period of tremendous company growth. She has received excellent reviews and raises along the way, but she struggles to balance it all, while trying to figure out how to move upward. Her dream is to be a CFO one day. She is newer to Intrinsic Work and has been using it for about a year.

"I'm a numbers gal," she tells me, "and I love what I do. But as I've grown my career I've found it tricky to balance—make that to *have* a personal life."

In addition to her own team and direct management, the accounting manager role requires her to be in contact with many people throughout the organization. There tends to be a lot of meetings, emails, and many other communication touches throughout the day. Additionally, this role demands a few forensic projects owned by Jennifer directly that she works on in-between everything else.

As a result, Jennifer tends to have "rapid fire" days. She works on her technical projects, while rapidly switching between emails that pop in, phone calls, texts, and engaging with people who stop by her office. This leads to lots of "high-touch, low-productivity" time in her workday.

Despite the madness, Jennifer gets her work done on time, usually by way of late nights and the occasional weekend. While she always gets her work done, she's never thrilled about burning the midnight oil, and longed for ways to keep work contained to the typical nine-to-five. However, that schedule looked more and more like a dream, since she needs fifty plus hours a week just to stay afloat, let alone, getting time for career growth and some semblance of a personal life.

"While Intrinsic has kicked me off to a great start," she says, "I've been high hours and really high performance, I'd like to get better control of it all while continuing my upward trajectory.

As she guided me into a seat in front of her desk and then walked around the desk to take hers, I noted how *quiet* her office was—a bit of a nice change from my time with Alan. I could actually hear a clock ticking as she smiled and said, "Okay, let's get started!"

Time Habits

When Jennifer was first introduced to Intrinsic Work she was intrigued. "What gets measured improves!" she says. "So I decided to *account for* a common workday and it looked like this before Intrinsic Work..."

- Step one was checking email, scanning for new projects, and adding them to the task list (30 minutes).

- Next, she went through her email again and answered all the ones asking for updates and needing responses. This could take a lot of time, and often by the time she finished, there were already responses and entirely new email chains to respond to. (2 hours).

- She noted that the two-hour period included several people walking up to her desk, asking for updates. Often, these were the same people she had already emailed back, and they hadn't looked at their emails yet. Once this was done she took a break to mentally prepare for starting her work (15 minutes).

- When she got back to her desk, she checked her email again, and answered all emails and added new tasks to her list (30 minutes).

- Then she got down to serious work on her projects (45 minutes).

- Then it was time for lunch (1 hour).

- When she got back from lunch she did the email loop again, answered questions, updated people on the progress of projects, and placed new tasks on the bottom of her task list (45 minutes).

- She then worked on her projects for 45 minutes …

- … until she had to leave for a cross functional team meeting (90 minutes).

- Afterward, she took a 15-minute break, and then got back and worked on her team project (90 minutes) until it was time to go home.

- She noted several start and stop points throughout the day , where she stopped to look at notifications on her phone and company messenger.

Like most office workers, Jennifer found that her day could be described using the "stock" Intrinsic framework. *Focused time*, *unfocused time*, *meetings* (lots of them) and some semblance of *downtime*. She was somewhat performing these time habits, just without any structure and with typical results. (Recall my old day verses ideal workday from Part 1.)

By calling out the time habits, it allowed Jennifer to be cognizant of them and to better define how they operate. For *focused time*, she created a *do-not-disturb* window on her email and phone. She bought a timer to help train herself away from occasional glances at her phone (this was difficult for her). After some trial and error she found *focused time* was best attempted first thing in the morning.

"I try to get a three-hour chunk of focused time from 9:00 a.m. to 12:00 p.m., take an hour lunch, and then bring on the chaos."

Jennifer lets people know about this scheduling routine and for the most part, people adjust their expectations.

Jennifer is still in the process of training herself and, most importantly, those around her. People still stop by unannounced, call when it's not important, and schedule meetings at whatever time they please. But it's getting better.

She would have to set boundaries on others with regard to her when and where. In her next round of meetings, during the time when coworkers are encouraged to talk about their challenges (which she normally found annoying) Jennifer raised her hand and let everyone know that she would be making progress updates at the end of each day. She asked that no one come to her desk for an update without first checking for her update email. And if they still had questions, "Please email me, or schedule a meeting, rather than stopping at my desk."

She would also need to set new boundaries for herself. Jennifer realized some of her wasted time was her own fault. She turned off notifications on her phone. She also asked her coworkers if they could discuss the shows they love over lunch, where they'd have more time, rather than making their breaks run over each morning. Then she had to STICK TO IT herself! She started nudging recurring meetings and events toward the chaos side of the day and grouped them together where possible.

"While not particularly pleasant, having my meetings back-to-back-to-back, allows me to be in attentive meeting mode for a while, and then I can switch back to office mode, be it more *focused time*, *unfocused time*, or just finishing off with the *daily close*."

She even eliminated a few meetings. "I transformed a weekly meeting into a monthly meeting, supplemented by a weekly email package, and in another weekly meeting, I replaced myself with the Senior Accountant who reports to me. They're enjoying the new exposure, and I have one less meeting every week, a win-win"

Big Goals

Like many people working their way up a corporate ladder, Jennifer's big goal is upper management, the C-suite, and for her lineage, Chief Financial Officer. Specifically, she wants to lead finance efforts for growth companies in clean energy (a pivot from her oil and gas background, though still in energy).

When considering what might be done in the upcoming year, *if she had the time*, Jennifer would like to get more involved with the forward-looking side of the business. As an accounting manager, she is well-exposed to history and reporting, "but this is everything that happened," and she would like to broaden her experience to "everything that should happen," which is generally the other leg of the CFO organization, opposite Accounting, Financial Planning, and Analysis.

Jennifer's boss agreed that these extracurricular goals could be pursued at her own pace and can live inside or outside the formal tracking system. Jennifer chose the first two to become part of her goals, while the last one would be informal to start. Corporate goals are annual measurement sticks that impact personal compensation, so she wanted to balance making her lofty goals informal versus formal.

Itemized

Big Goal
Achieve CFO while still enjoying a personal life.
Component Goals
1. **Continued success at current gig.** Learn the finance side of the business.

2. **Success elsewhere**. Lead finance efforts for a growth company in alternative energy (a pivot from oil and gas, but still in energy).
3. **Create more personal time** via better efficiency at work.

Annual Goals ~ Continued Success at Current Gig

A. **FP&A Connect**: Work cross-functionally with FP&A to capture and plan operating expenses. In the process, learn more about their side of the world and find material dollar reductions.
B. **Strategy Transaction**: Work with Sales on a Master Service Agreement ("MSA") with one of three new customers currently in the pipeline. Rather than accounting for the transaction after the fact, she will work with Sales up front on contract language, economics, and execution.
C. **One-Day Close**: While expanding outside her sphere with the above is great, mastering her organization will make her life easier while demonstrating resume-building excellence. The gold standard is to properly close books with a one-day close. This results in faster reporting but is also a measurement of efficiency. The data must be timely and accurate with robust processes and balanced controls.

Annual Goals ~ Pivot to Energy Startup

A. **Research** alternative energy sectors. There are many options, from nuclear to solar to wind. Form a preference.
B. **Update resume**, with a slant toward alternative energy and startups. Highlight financial processes I've built, not just operated.

C. **Find recruiters** in the space, have conversations. Gain more knowledge, get to know the industry while you are still gainfully employed.

Annual Goals ~ Create More Personal Time

A. **Push the Intrinsic Work Framework:** Intrinsic Work is essentially an instruction manual. Revisit how things are going often, make adjustments to the current work situation for better efficiency while still accomplishing all you have been doing and more.

Levered Tasks Example for One Annual Goal

With the goals outlined above, Jennifer also spoke to her boss and the heads of Sales and FP&A about her plans. They were all intrigued by her ideas. Below is her Goal/Time/Task mapping for her *annual goal* of *FP&A Connect.*

Levered Tasks	Time Habits			
	Focused Time	**Unfocused Time**	**Meetings**	**Downtime**
Annual Goal: FP&A Connect	Research best practices in financial forecasting.	Email Glen in FP&A for materials/current process.	Recurring weekly 30-min to propose, feedback, and hone plan.	Lunch with head of FP&A and boss once per quarter.
	Learn current process.	Schedule recurring meetings and lunches.	Define implementation meeting(s) as identified.	
	Design potential alternatives (uplevel).			

Her tasks are designed to guide and focus her efforts. They don't necessarily document every little detail and motion, but they are the broad pieces to keep her daily efforts on track.

Jennifer's Driving Momentum

Daily Planning

Jennifer deployed a number of tactics from **Part 4: Drive Momentum**. She prints and plans her *Super Day* the day before every workday. On Monday, she preps Tuesday, and on Friday, she preps Monday. She always has a good sense of what's going on the next day.

Super Day

Jennifer has used and still loves her *Super Days.*

SUPER DAY

MAXIMUM PRODUCTIVITY: ACHIEVE MORE, WORK LESS, AND ENJOY LIFE!

Time Habit	Start Time	Minutes	Goals & Tasks (circled when done)	Done?
Unfocused	8:00 a.m.	30:00	• Daily commute to Longview. • *Current audiobook = The CFO Mind: Making Your Career Count.*	yes
Unfocused	8:30 a.m.	30:00	• Arrive at office. • "Watercooler/coffee" time with co-workers, emphasis on relevant/useful conversations or simply socialization with staff.	yes
Focused	9:00 a.m	3 hours	• Bookkeeping! • Any forensic projects in-progress. • Preparation of statements and reports for management.	yes
Lunch	12:00 p.m.	60:00	• *Main concern = healthy lunch prepared from home, includes 15 minutes of "closed door" meditation.*	yes
Unfocused	1:00 p.m.	30:00	• More "watercooler/coffee" time with office staff, as this is often combined with informal requests and reports (I've found by scheduling this it no longer gets splattered all over my day).	yes
Meeting	1:30 p.m.	60:00	• Ad-hoc meeting with operations to discuss purchase order approval process that is not working.	
Focused	2:30 p.m.	90:00	• More bookkeeping! • Any payroll tasks, state + federal reporting, etc. • Other current projects.	yes
Meeting	4:00 p.m.	60:00	• *We have a rather long meeting at the end of each day which after evaluation does seem relevant but more importantly is currently required by CEO.*	yes
Close	5:00 p.m.	15:00	• Comb emails, update the Super List, Plan + print next *Super Day*	yes
Unfocused	5:15 p.m	30:00	• *Drive home: Current listen = various audiobooks and podcasts on time management and organizational efficiency to achieve more production and personal time.*	IP

The Drive Home

Jennifer's drive home of roughly 30 minutes is now vital time invested in knowledge that will advance her career and just as importantly, continue to educate her into more and better ways of managing her already-scarce time. She reports that, "by doing this I really feel like I'm making progress for me, not just the company, and as Abraham Lincoln said, I think, 'If I had one hour to cut down a tree I'd spend 30 minutes sharpening my axe,' or something like that."

Accountability

Her accountability partner is her friend from an earlier job. Before becoming an accounting manager, Jennifer was an auditor for one of the big audit firms. At the firm, you work grueling hours for low compensation in exchange for amazing experience. On the inside, there is a chance at making "partner" and great career opportunities on the outside as you move up.

"It's like a rocket ship for your career" she says. The only problem is you're strapped to the outside of it."

Comradery at the firm was great. Jennifer searched for potential accountability partners based on her LinkedIn connections and got in contact with a few people. One was a former co-worker who was still at the firm, and the other was a partner at the firm, who left to be a CFO at a public company.

Her former co-worker is now an audit senior manager, which is roughly the same level as Jennifer's well-experienced accounting manager role. They meet on a weekly basis, either by Zoom or for lunch. Turns out the firm has a "charge code" that pays for lunch, when you take former colleagues out to lunch (it's a new business strategy). The CFO she talks to on a semi-regular basis, just three to four times per year, but it has made plenty of impact on her career decisions.

Helpful Tools

- Jennifer relies on her task list, and enjoys checking off pieces of it, and updating it as she learns new information and reprioritizes. Sometimes a newly discovered task related to a goal will slot ahead of something she thought she was going to do the next day. She enjoys being able to re-prioritize and shift focus day-to-day. She maintains her tasks in Excel, but I've encouraged her to get them into the Intrinsic application.

- She deploys the **Super Week** as a check-off list. She prints it and magnets it to her whiteboard, which is eye level on the wall next to her. At the end of each day, she circles whether the time habit was done successfully. Sometimes they aren't and that's okay. Measure what matters and try again the next day.

- Additionally, when preparing for her Super Week, she blocks her calendar the following week for any time habits that are not already accounted for. This allows for more meeting availability leading up to the week, and then less availability during the week.

- She tied her personal and digital calendars together to make "at a glance" scheduling easier. She also requested that her husband send her an invite for anything and everything. "If it gets on my calendar, I'm on it!"

- Finally, the sub-system she uses at work is an Excel workbook which she calls "Finance Everything." It contains historical numbers that are good to have at hand. It has reminders about various people, including key people inside the company, vendor and customers she's met, bankers, and all sorts of other people whose name and notes are good to have available. It has a tab for her goals and tasks that are outlined here. It has custom tools and auto-checkers that she has developed to help with the monthly close process. This Excel workbook is her one-stop for everything finance at her company, as it relates to her role and beyond it. It makes it much easier to keep track of everything and find everything.

Jennifer, how's it going?

Jennifer has been working on the **Intrinsic System** for nearly a year. Initially, she struggled with long-duration **focused time** for all the usual reasons. First, she had to train herself. "It was hard staying on task, worrying about missing out on the inbox, the cellphone, and perhaps social media" she said.

Today, she uses her timer less often, because she can walk into the office and dive into her whole three-hour time slot. If anything, she uses it when her **focused time** is shorter, so she doesn't miss her meeting or whatever is interrupting it. Not only has she trained herself, she's trained those around her, for the most part.

People still schedule meetings where she doesn't want them, stop by unannounced, and otherwise derail her plans. And that's okay. It happens much less than it used to, allowing her to still achieve much higher productivity with her workdays.

Speaking of those workdays, Jennifer no longer works evenings and weekends. In fact, some might say she pushes the boundaries on her work's "unlimited PTO" policy. She gets so much done on a day-to-day basis that she can simply let go more often.

As for her trajectory, after a year of gaining FP&A experience she made the switch. After defining her just right "goldilocks role" she went looking for it.

It took three months of looking to checkoff exactly what she wanted:

1. A well-funded alternative energy company with established leadership.

2. A role that was hybrid or entirely work from home.

3. A role that pays well and is an obvious trajectory toward CFO, on the finance side.

She is now the VP of Finance at a prominent alternative energy startup, reporting to the CEO. Both the accounting and finance functions report to her. The role pays well, it is remote, and if she plays her cards right, the CFO slot can be hers. The company hopes to go public within a couple of years, at which point the board will hire a highly experienced outside CFO or promote her to the spot. The way she sees it, there is upside either way.

Closing Motivation

YOU CAN DO this! You can have a more productive work life and use it however you'd like.

- Big career? No problem.

- Make work easy? Done.

- Do something else entirely? You got it.

- Maybe even some blended trajectory.

Implementing any piece of this system will improve your life, while all pieces will improve your life exponentially. Here's a recap of some of the IMMEDIATE ACTIONS/FIRST STEPS that can be taken to get work running smoothly:

#1 – Time habits
- Schedule *focused time* and other *time habits* for tomorrow in the *Super Day* format.
- Consider ways to make your environment more comfortable.
- Train yourself not to be distracted during *focused time.*

#2 – Big goal setting

- Define your *long-term goal* – climbing, mastering, or changing in nature.
- Break it into three *component goals*, including success at current company.
- Break each one into three *annual goals.*

#3 – Levered task planning

- Write out all your work tasks for your *annual goals* and other responsibilities.
- Add "Other" *annual goals* for topics that don't fit. Everything must go on the Task List.
- Identify what you might delegate, automate, or otherwise get off your plate.
- Uplevel your tasks with research.

#4 – Drive momentum

- Plan a *Super Day* with *levered tasks* for tomorrow.
- Plan your *Super Week.*
- Write out a people list and find an accountability partner.
- Define how you'll use your calendar, lists, and notes.
- Identify Supporting Systems as needed.
- Consider implementing helpful psychologies, such as Flow State, Counterbalancing, CCRR, Big Gestures, It's okay to Say No!, and The Simulator.

Our templates and application can help. You can find them at MyIntrinsicWork.com.

Let's be real…

Setting this up is "easy." Implementing it takes time.

Your environment will need to be nudged, and you'll need to be nudged as well. Squashing work into a highly productive tiny footprint won't happen overnight. But *attempting to* structure it *will* structure it, and you'll get there incrementally.

As you nudge meetings toward your preferred cluster and as you become more schedule-cognizant, time will better slot into place. My day doesn't always go as planned—but it's almost always productive and pushing in the right direction.

Goals can restrict happiness by creating the "I'll be happy when I achieve XYZ" mindset. Having great systems running means you know where you're heading. The journey itself promotes happiness, and the phrase subtlety changes to "I'm happy when I'm working to achieve XYZ."

Be kind to yourself along the way.

You won't always get there 100% of the time. If you miss, get back to it the next workday. That is the important part: MAKE SURE YOU GET BACK TO IT. If you stick with the system, goal-oriented decisions will come naturally, and being highly organized will be an afterthought. You'll be a high performer and can use it to achieve more, work less, and enjoy life.

Beyond Intrinsic Work:
Intrinsic Life

THIS BOOK IS specifically designed for deep application related to managing work. The next book is much broader, applying our techniques to life. Below is the suggestive starter framework.

Time Habits expand to include:

1. Focused time (200 days per year speed limit)

2. Unfocused time

3. Meetings

4. Downtime (breakfast, lunch, dinner, breaks)

5. Technical learning

6. Interesting learning

7. Reading

8. Walking

9. Exercise

10. Meditation

11. Quality time (outings, vacations, etc.)

Big goal categories and components expand to include things important to you. Below are mine:

1. **Spiritual**
   a. Faith
   b. Consciousness
   c. Habits
2. **Health**
   a. Physical
   b. Mental
3. **Personal Life**
   a. Hobbies
   b. Romance
   c. Children
4. **Relationships**
   a. Family
   b. Friends
   c. Professional
5. **Work**
   a. Current Company
   b. Next role

    c.   Something new

6. **Business**

    a.   Replace Work

    b.   Humanitarian

    c.   Politics

7. **Finances**

    a.   Household budget

    b.   Consume Effectively

    c.   Buy Cool Stuff

The top-level framework comes from *The One Thing: The Surprisingly Simple Truth About Extraordinary Results*, authored by Gary Keller and Jay Papasan. The goals are numbered in the order of importance that they should consume in your life. That's right. This entire book has been dedicated to the 5th most important aspect of your life.

The ***component goals*** are my creations. Most are obvious, though you might fine-tune them for yourself. There are annual goals that branch from there. MyIntrinsicLife.com will have more information and supporting materials.

Thank you,
Andrew

About the Author

ANDREW CAMP has always been a worker. Here's the list:

- Nicolino's Italian Restaurant
- In-N-Out Burger
- Best Buy
- CompUSA
- Kaiser Hospital
- Deloitte
- GitHub
- Enphase Energy
- Recology
- Sunfolding
- Enzinc

Along the way he graduated high school, spent six years on an associate's degree and had a child. Earned a bachelor's degree, got married, earned an MBA, and year after that, finally got his first professional job at Deloitte. While there he had another child, and eventually left audit life for GitHub. That was a lot. Afterwards he slowed down a bit, with a handful of moves between escalating corporate finance roles.

He lives in Petaluma, CA, with his wife, two kids and their goldendoodle. Andrew enjoys fast cars, good music, and vacations with the family. And being wildly productive, which these days, he uses to work less.

Congratulations!

You are on your way to being more productive.

Use it to achieve more, work less and enjoy life!

Make this even easier with the Intrinsic Work application. Our app puts your life management in digital form.

Like QuickBooks for most businesses, our app is designed to help most people manage their lives.

Check it out for free at

www.MyIntrinsicWork.com

While there, send me a message. I love to hear about your progress and struggles. It's hard out there, keep the momentum going!

Best,

Andrew